Fashion, Costume, *and* Culture

Clothing, Headwear, Body Decorations, and Footwear through the Ages

Fashion, Costume, *and* Culture

Clothing, Headwear, Body Decorations, and Footwear through the Ages

Volume 3:
**European Culture
from the Renaissance
to the Modern Era**

SARA PENDERGAST AND TOM PENDERGAST

SARAH HERMSEN, *Project Editor*

Detroit • New York • San Diego • San Francisco • Cleveland • New Haven, Conn. • Waterville, Maine • London • Munich

THOMSON
GALE

Fashion, Costume, and Culture: Clothing, Headwear, Body Decorations, and Footwear through the Ages

Sara Pendergast and Tom Pendergast

Project Editor
Sarah Hermsen

Editorial
Lawrence W. Baker

Permissions
Shalice Shah-Caldwell, Ann Taylor

Imaging and Multimedia
Dean Dauphinais, Dave Oblender

Product Design
Kate Scheible

Composition
Evi Seoud

Manufacturing
Rita Wimberley

For permission to use material from this product, submit your request via the Web at http://www.gale-edit.com/permissions, or you may download our Permissions Request form and submit your request by fax or mail to:

Permissions Department
The Gale Group, Inc.
27500 Drake Rd.
Farmington Hills, MI 48331-3535
Permissions Hotline:
248-699-8006 or 800-877-4253, ext. 8006
Fax: 248-699-8074 or 800-762-4058

Cover photographs reproduced by permission of: Volume 1, from top to bottom, © Christel Gerstenberg/CORBIS, AP/Wide World Photos, © Araldo de Luca/CORBIS; large photo, the Library of Congress. Volume 2, from top to bottom, Public Domain, © Gianni Dagli Orti/CORBIS, National Archives and Records Administration; large photo, the Smithsonian Institute. Volume 3, from top to bottom, © Historical

Picture Archive/CORBIS, the Library of Congress, AP/Wide World Photos; large photo, Public Domain. Volume 4, from top to bottom, © Austrian Archives/CORBIS, AP/Wide World Photos, © Kelly A. Quin; large photo, AP/Wide World Photos. Volume 5, from top to bottom, Susan D. Rock, AP/Wide World Photos, © Ken Settle; large photo, AP/Wide World Photos.

While every effort has been made to ensure the reliability of the information presented in this publication, The Gale Group, Inc. does not guarantee the accuracy of data contained herein. The Gale Group, Inc. accepts no payment for listing; and inclusion in the publication of any organization, agency, institution, publication, service, or individual does not imply endorsement by the editors or publisher. Errors brought to the attention of the publisher and verified to the satisfaction of the publisher will be corrected in future editions.

LIBRARY OF CONGRESS CATALOGING-IN-PUBLICATION DATA

Pendergast, Sara.
Fashion, costume, and culture: clothing, headwear, body decorations, and footwear through the ages / Sara Pendergast and Tom Pendergast; Sarah Hermsen, editor.
 p. cm.
Includes bibliographical references and index.
ISBN 0-7876-5417-5 (set hardcover)—ISBN 0-7876-5418-3 (v.1 : alk. paper)—ISBN 0-7876-5419-1 (v.2 : alk. paper)—ISBN 0-7876-5420-5 (v.3 : alk. paper)—ISBN 0-7876-5421-3 (v.4 : alk. paper)— ISBN 0-7876-5422-1 (v.5 : alk. paper)
1. Costume—History. 2. Fashion—History. 3. Body marking—History. 4. Dress accessories—History. I. Title: Clothing, headwear, body decorations, and footwear through the ages. II. Pendergast, Tom. III. Hermsen, Sarah. IV. Title. GT511.P46 2004
391'.009—dc22
                                    2003015852

Contents

■■■

■
■
■ *Volume 1:* The Ancient World

PREHISTORY

ANCIENT EGYPT

■
■
■ *Volume 2:* Early Cultures
■   Across the Globe

EARLY ASIAN CULTURES

AFRICAN CULTURES

■
■
■ *Volume 3:* European Culture from
the Renaissance to the Modern Era

THE FIFTEENTH CENTURY

THE SIXTEENTH CENTURY

Volume 4: Modern World
Part I: 1900 to 1945

1900–18

Clothing

Headwear

Body Decorations

Footwear

Volume 5: Modern World
Part II: 1946 to 2003

Entries by Alphabetical Order

A

B

C

D

E

F

‖ G

‖ H

I

J

K

L

M

N

O

P

R

S

T

U

V

W

Z

Entries by Topic Category

Clothing

‖ Headwear

▌ Body Decorations

‖ Footwear

Reader's Guide

■ ■ ■

Fashion, Costume, and Culture: Clothing, Headwear, Body Decorations, and Footwear through the Ages provides a broad overview of costume traditions of diverse cultures from prehistoric times to the present day. The five-volume set explores various items of human decoration and adornment, ranging from togas to turbans, necklaces to tennis shoes, and discusses why and how they were created, the people who made them, and their uses. More than just a description of what people wore and why, this set also describes how clothing, headwear, body decorations, and footwear reflect different cultural, religious, and societal beliefs.

Volume 1 covers the ancient world, including prehistoric man and the ancient cultures of Egypt, Mesopotamia, India, Greece, and Rome. Key issues covered in this volume include the early use of animal skins as garments, the introduction of fabric as the primary human body covering, and the development of distinct cultural traditions for draped and fitted garments.

Volume 2 looks at the transition from the ancient world to the Middle Ages, focusing on the Asian cultures of China and Japan, the Byzantine Empire, the nomadic and barbarian cultures of early Europe, and Europe in the formative Middle Ages. This volume also highlights several of the ancient cultures of North America, South and Central America, and Africa that were encountered by

Europeans during the Age of Exploration that began in the fifteenth century.

Volumes 3 through 5 offer chronological coverage of the development of costume and fashion in the West. Volume 3 features the costume traditions of the developing European nation-states in the fifteenth through the nineteenth centuries, and looks at the importance of the royal courts in introducing clothing styles and the shift from home-based garmentmaking to shop-based and then factory-based industry.

Volumes 4 and 5 cover the period of Western history since 1900. These volumes trace the rise of the fashion designer as the primary creator of new clothing styles, chart the impact of technology on costume traditions, and present the innovations made possible by the introduction of new synthetic, or man-made, materials. Perhaps most importantly, Volumes 4 and 5 discuss what is sometimes referred to as the democratization of fashion. At the beginning of the twentieth century, high quality, stylish clothes were designed by and made available to a privileged elite; by the middle to end of the century, well-made clothes were widely available in the West, and new styles came from creative and usually youth-oriented cultural groups as often as they did from designers.

Organization

Fashion, Costume, and Culture is organized into twenty-five chapters, focusing on specific cultural traditions or on a specific chronological period in history. Each of these chapters share the following components:

- A chapter introduction, which discusses the general historical framework for the chapter and highlights the major social and economic factors that relate to the development of costume traditions.

- Four sections that cover Clothing, Headwear, Body Decorations, and Footwear. Each of these sections opens with an overview that discusses general trends within the broader category, and nearly every section contains one or more essays on specific garments or trends that were important during the period.

Each chapter introduction and individual essay in *Fashion, Costume, and Culture* includes a For More Information section listing sources—books, articles, and Web sites—containing additional information on fashion and the people and events it addresses. Some essays also contain *See also* references that direct the reader to other essays within the set that can offer more information on this or related items.

Bringing the text to life are more than 330 color or black-and-white photos and maps, while numerous sidebar boxes offer additional insight into the people, places, and happenings that influenced fashion throughout the years. Other features include tables of contents listing the contents of all five volumes, listing the entries by alphabetical order, and listing entries by category. Rounding out the set are a timeline of important events in fashion history, a words to know section defining terms used throughout the set, a bibliography of general fashion sources, including notable Web sites, and a comprehensive subject index, which provides easy access to the subjects discussed throughout *Fashion, Costume, and Culture.*

Acknowledgments

Many thanks to the following advisors who provided valuable comments and suggestions for *Fashion, Costume, and Culture:* Ginny Chaussee, Retired Media Specialist, Mountain Pointe High School, Phoenix, Arizona; Carol Keeler, Media Specialist, Detroit Country Day Upper School, Beverly Hills, Michigan; Nina Levine, Library Media Specialist, Blue Mountain Middle School, Cortlandt Manor, New York; and Bonnie Raasch, Media Specialist, C. B. Vernon Middle School, Marion, Iowa.

No work of this size could be completed without the efforts of many dedicated people. The authors would like to thank Sarah Hermsen, who shouldered the work of picture selection and ushered the book through copyediting and production. She deserves a good share of the credit for the success of this project. We also owe a great deal to the writers who have helped us create the hundreds of essays in this book: Tina Gianoulis, Rob Edelman, Bob Schnakenberg, Audrey Kupferberg, and Carol Brennan. The staff at U•X•L has been a pleasure to work with, and Carol Nagel and Tom Romig deserve special mention for the cheerfulness and professionalism they bring to their work. We'd also like to thank the staffs of two libraries, at the University of Washington and the Sno-Isle Regional Library, for allowing us to ransack and hold hostage their costume collections for months at a time.

We cannot help but mention the great debt we owe to the costume historians whose works we have consulted, and whose names appear again and again in the bibliographies of the essays. We sincerely hope that this collection pays tribute to and furthers their collective production of knowledge.

—Sara Pendergast and Tom Pendergast

Comments and Suggestions

We welcome your comments on *Fashion, Costume, and Culture* as well as your suggestions for topics to be featured in future editions. Please write to: Editor, *Fashion, Costume, and Culture,* U•X•L, 27500 Drake Road, Farmington Hills, Michigan, 48331-3535; call toll-free: 800-877-4253; fax to 248-414-5043; or send e-mail via http://www.gale.com.

Contributors

■ ■ ■

CAROL BRENNAN. Freelance Writer, Grosse Pointe, MI.

ROB EDELMAN. Instructor, State University of New York at Albany. Author, *Baseball on the Web* (1997) and *The Great Baseball Films* (1994). Co-author, *Matthau: A Life* (2002); *Meet the Mertzes* (1999); and *Angela Lansbury: A Life on Stage and Screen* (1996). Contributing editor, *Leonard Maltin's Move & Video Guide, Leonard Maltin's Movie Encyclopedia,* and *Leonard Maltin's Family Viewing Guide.* Contributing writer, *International Dictionary of Films and Filmmakers* (2000); *St. James Encyclopedia of Popular Culture* (2000); *Women Filmmakers & Their Films* (1998); *The Political Companion to American Film* (1994); and *Total Baseball* (1989). Film commentator, WAMC (Northeast) Public Radio.

TINA GIANOULIS. Freelance Writer. Contributing writer, *World War I Reference Library* (2002); *Constitutional Amendments: From Freedom of Speech to Flag Burning* (2001); *International Dictionary of Films and Filmmakers* (2000); *St. James Encyclopedia of Popular Culture* (2000); and mystories.com, a daytime drama Web site (1997–98).

AUDREY KUPFERBERG. Film consultant and archivist. Instructor, State University of New York at Albany. Co-author, *Matthau: A Life* (2002); *Meet the Mertzes* (1999); and *Angela Lansbury: A Life on Stage and Screen* (1996). Contributing editor, *Leonard Maltin's*

Family Viewing Guide. Contributing writer, *St. James Encyclopedia of Popular Culture* (2000). Editor, *Rhythm* (2001), a magazine of world music and global culture.

SARA PENDERGAST. President, Full Circle Editorial. Vice president, Group 3 Editorial. Co-editor, *St. James Encyclopedia of Popular Culture* (2000). Co-author, *World War I Reference Library* (2002), among other publications.

TOM PENDERGAST. Editorial director, Full Circle Editorial. Ph.D., American studies, Purdue University. Author, *Creating the Modern Man: American Magazines and Consumer Culture* (2000). Co-editor, *St. James Encyclopedia of Popular Culture* (2000).

ROBERT E. SCHNAKENBERG. Senior writer, History Book Club. Author, *The Encyclopedia Shatnerica* (1998).

Timeline

■ ■ ■

THE BEGINNING OF HUMAN LIFE ■ Early humans wrap themselves in animal hides for warmth.

c. 10,000 B.C.E. ■ Tattooing is practiced on the Japanese islands, in the Jomon period (c. 10,000–300 B.C.E.). Similarly scarification, the art of carving designs into the skin, has been practiced since ancient times in Oceania and Africa to make a person's body more beautiful or signify a person's rank in society.

c. 3100 B.C.E. ■ Egyptians weave a plant called flax into a light cloth called linen and made dresses and loincloths from it.

c. 3100 B.C.E. ■ Egyptians shave their heads to keep themselves clean and cool in the desert heat, but covered their heads with wigs of various styles.

c. 10,000 B.C.E. Humans populated most of the major landmasses on Earth	**c. 7000 B.C.E.** The first human settlements were developed in Mesopotamia
■	■
10,000 B.C.E.	**7000 B.C.E.**

c. 3100 B.C.E. ■ Egyptians perfume their bodies by coating their skin in fragrant oils and ointments.

c. 3000 B.C.E. ■ Men and women in the Middle East, Africa, and the Far East have wrapped turbans on their heads since ancient times, and the turban continues to be popular with both men and women in many modern cultures.

c. 2600 B.C.E. TO 900 C.E. ■ Ancient Mayans, whose civilization flourishes in Belize and on the Yucatan Peninsula in Mexico, flatten the heads of the children of wealthy and powerful members of society. The children's heads are squeezed between two boards to elongate their skulls into a shape that looks very similar to an ear of corn.

c. 2500 B.C.E. ■ Indians wear a wrapped style of trousers called a dhoti and a skirt-like lower body covering called a lungi.

c. 2500 B.C.E. ■ Indian women begin to adorn themselves in the wrapped dress style called a sari.

c. 1500 B.C.E. ■ Egyptian men adopt the tunic as an upper body covering when Egypt conquers Syria.

c. 27 B.C.E.–476 C.E. ■ Roman soldiers, especially horsemen, adopt the trousers, or feminalia, of the nomadic tribes they encounter on the outskirts of the Roman Empire.

SIXTH AND FIFTH CENTURIES B.C.E. ■ The doric chiton becomes one of the most popular garments for both men and women in ancient Greece.

FIFTH CENTURY B.C.E. ■ The toga, a wrapped garment, is favored by Romans.

c. 3500 B.C.E.	c. 2680–2526 B.C.E.	c. 1792–1750 B.C.E.	**44 B.C.E.**
Beginnings of Sumerian civilization	Building of the Great Pyramids near Giza, Egypt	Hammurabi creates empire of Babylonia	Julius Caesar becomes Roman dictator for life and is then assassinated
■	■	■	■

4000 B.C.E.	3000 B.C.E.	2000 B.C.E.	1000 B.C.E.

c. 476 ■ Upper-class men, and sometimes women, in the Byzantine Empire (476–1453 C.E.) wear a long, flowing robe-like overgarment called a dalmatica developed from the tunic.

c. 900 ■ Young Chinese girls tightly bind their feet to keep them small, a sign of beauty for a time in Chinese culture. The practice was outlawed in 1911.

c. 1100–1500 ■ The cote, a long robe worn by both men and women, and its descendant, the cotehardie, are among the most common garments of the late Middle Ages.

1392 ■ Kimonos are first worn in China as an undergarment. The word "kimono" later came to be used to describe the native dress of Japan in the nineteenth century.

MIDDLE AGES ■ Hose and breeches, which cover the legs individually, become more common garments for men.

FOURTEENTH CENTURY TO SIXTEENTH CENTURY ■ Cuts and openings in garments made from slashing and dagging decorate garments from upper body coverings to shoes.

1470 ■ The first farthingales, or hoops worn under a skirt to hold it out away from the body, are worn in Spain and are called vertugados. These farthingales become popular in France and England and are later known as the Spanish farthingale.

FIFTEENTH CENTURY AND SIXTEENTH CENTURY ■ The doublet—a slightly padded short overshirt, usually buttoned down the front, with or without sleeves—becomes an essential men's garment.

330 Constantine I names Constantinople as capital city of Byzantine Empire	710 Sugar is planted in Egypt	1016 Viking Canute I, the Great begins rule as king of England, Denmark, and Norway	1421 Mohammed I dies
■	■	■	■
350 C.E.	**700** C.E.	**1050** C.E.	**1400** C.E.

LATE FIFTEENTH THROUGH THE SIXTEENTH CENTURY ■ The ruff, a wide pleated collar, often stiffened with starch or wire, is worn by wealthy men and women of the time.

SIXTEENTH CENTURY ■ Worn underneath clothing, corsets squeeze and mold women's bodies into the correct shape to fit changing fashions of dress.

SIXTEENTH CENTURY ■ People carry or wear small pieces of animal fur in hopes that biting fleas will be more attracted to the animal's skin than to their own.

LATE MIDDLE AGES ■ The beret, a soft, brimless wool hat, is the most popular men's hat during the late Middle Ages and into the fifteenth and sixteenth centuries, especially in France, Italy, and Spain.

1595 ■ Europeans land on the Marquesas Islands in Oceania and discover native inhabitants covered in tattoos.

SEVENTEENTH CENTURY ■ The Kuba people, living in the present-day nation of the Democratic Republic of the Congo, weave a decorative cloth called Kuba cloth. An entire social group of men and women is involved in the production of the cloth, from gathering the fibers, weaving the cloth, and dyeing the decorative strands, to applying the embroidery, appliqué, or patchwork.

SEVENTEENTH CENTURY ■ Canes become carefully crafted items and are carried by most well-dressed gentleman.

1643 ■ French courtiers begin wearing wigs to copy the long curly hair of the sixteen-year-old king, Louis XIV. The fashion for long wigs continues later when, at the age of thirty-five, Louis begins to cover his thinning hair with wigs to maintain his beloved style.

1502	1558	1618	1643
First slaves are shipped to the New World	Elizabeth I begins her forty-five-year reign as queen of England	Thirty Years' War begins	Louis XIV is crowned king of France
■	■	■	■
1500	**1550**	**1600**	**1650**

EIGHTEENTH CENTURY ■ French men tuck flowers in the buttonholes of their waistcoats and introduce boutonières as fashionable nosegays for men.

EIGHTEENTH CENTURY ■ The French Revolution (1789–99) destroys the French monarchy and makes ankle-length trousers fashionable attire for all men. Trousers come to symbolize the ideas of the Revolution, an effort to make French people more equal, and soon men of all classes are wearing long trousers.

1778 ■ À la Belle Poule, a huge hairstyle commemorating the victory of a French ship over an English ship in 1778, features an enormous pile of curled and powdered hair stretched over a frame affixed to the top of a woman's head. The hair is decorated with a model of the ship in full sail.

1849 ■ Dark blue, heavy-duty cotton pants—known as blue jeans— are created as work pants for the gold miners of the 1849 California gold rush.

1868 ■ A sturdy canvas and rubber shoe called a croquet sandal is introduced and sells for six dollars a pair, making it too expensive for all but the very wealthy. The shoe later became known as the tennis shoe.

1870 ■ A French hairstylist named Marcel Grateau invents the first long-lasting hair waving technique using a heated iron to give hair curls that lasts for days.

LATE 1800s TO EARLY 1900s ■ The feathered war bonnet, traditional to only a small number of Native American tribes, becomes known as a typical Native American headdress with the help of Buffalo Bill Cody's Wild West Show, which features theatrical representations of the Indians and cowboys of the American West and travels throughout America and parts of Europe.

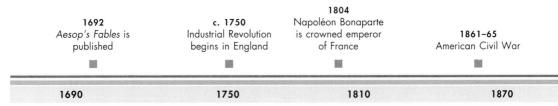

1692	c. 1750	1804	1861–65
Aesop's Fables is published	Industrial Revolution begins in England	Napoléon Bonaparte is crowned emperor of France	American Civil War
■	■	■	■
1690	1750	1810	1870

1900s ■ Loose, floppy, two-legged undergarments for women, bloomers start a trend toward less restrictive clothing for women, including clothing that allows them to ride bicycles, play tennis, and to take part in other sport activities.

1915 ■ American inventor T.L. Williams develops a cake of mascara and a brush to darken the lashes and sells them through the mail under the name Maybelline.

1920s ■ Advances in paint technology allow the creation of a hard durable paint and fuel an increase in the popularity of colored polish for fingernails and toenails.

1920s ■ The navy blue blazer, a jacket with brass buttons, becomes popular for men to wear at sporting events.

1920s ■ A fad among women for wearing short, bobbed hairstyles sweeps America and Europe.

1930s ■ Popular as a shirt for tennis, golf, and other sport activities for decades, the polo shirt becomes the most popular leisure shirt for men.

1939 ■ For the first time, *Vogue,* the respected fashion magazine, pictures women in trousers.

1945 ■ Servicemen returning home from World War II (1939–45) continue to wear the T-shirts they had been issued as undershirts during the war and soon the T-shirt becomes an acceptable casual outershirt.

1946 ■ The bikini, a two-piece bathing suit, is developed and named after a group of coral islands in the Pacific Ocean.

1950s ■ The gray flannel suit becomes the most common outfit worn by men working at desk jobs in office buildings.

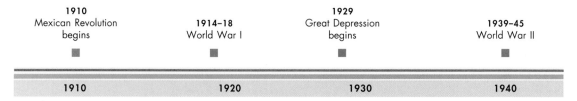

1910 Mexican Revolution begins	1914–18 World War I	1929 Great Depression begins	1939–45 World War II
■	■	■	■
1910	1920	1930	1940

1957 ■ Liquid mascara is sold at retail stores in tubes with a brush inside.

1960s AND 1970s ■ The afro, featuring a person's naturally curly hair trimmed in a full, evenly round shape around the head, is the most popular hairstyle among African Americans.

c. 1965 ■ Women begin wearing miniskirts with hemlines hitting at mid-thigh or above.

1980s ■ Power dressing becomes a trend toward wearing expensive, designer clothing for work.

1990s ■ Casual Fridays becomes the name given to the practice of allowing employees to dress informally on the last day of the work week.

1990s ■ Grunge, a trend for wearing old, sometimes stained or ripped clothing, becomes a fashion sensation and prompts designers to sell simple flannel shirts for prices in excess of one thousand dollars.

2000s ■ Versions of clothing available during the 1960s and 1970s, such as bell-bottom jeans and the peasant look, return to fashion as "retro fashions."

1947 Jawaharlal Nehru becomes the first prime minister of an independent India	**1963** U.S. president John F. Kennedy is assassinated	**1989** Berlin Wall falls	**2001** Terrorists attack the World Trade Center and the Pentagon
■	■	■	■
1945	**1965**	**1985**	**2005**

Words to Know

■ ■ ■

 A

Appliqué: An ornament sewn, embroidered, or glued onto a garment.

 B

Bias cut: A fabric cut diagonally across the weave to create a softly draped garment.

Bodice: The part of a woman's garment that covers her torso from neck to waist.

Bombast: Padding used to increase the width or add bulk to the general silhouette of a garment.

Brim: The edge of a hat that projects outward away from the head.

Brocade: A fabric woven with a raised pattern over the entire surface.

C

Collar: The part of a shirt that surrounds the neck.

Crown: The portion of a hat that covers the top of the head; may also refer to the top part of the head.

Cuff: A piece of fabric sewn at the bottom of a sleeve.

 D

Double-breasted: A style of jacket in which one side (usually the left) overlaps in the front of the other side, fastens at the waist with a vertical row of buttons, and has another row of buttons on the opposite side that is purely decorative. *See also* Single-breasted.

 E

Embroidery: Needlework designs on the surface of a fabric, added for decoration.

 G

Garment: Any article of clothing.

 H

Hemline: The bottom edge of a skirt, jacket, dress, or other garment.

Hide: The pelt of an animal with the fur intact.

 I

Instep: The upper surface of the arched middle portion of the human foot in front of the ankle joint.

Jersey: A knitted fabric usually made of wool or cotton.

Lapel: One of the two flaps that extend down from the collar of a coat or jacket and fold back against the chest.

Lasts: The foot-shaped forms or molds that are used to give shape to shoes in the process of shoemaking.

Leather: The skin or hide of an animal cleaned and treated to soften it and preserve it from decay.

Linen: A fabric woven from the fibers of the flax plant. Linen was one of the first woven fabrics.

Mule: A shoe without a covering or strap around the heel of the foot.

Muslin: A thin cotton fabric.

Patent Leather: Leather varnished and buffed to a high shine.

Placket: A slit in a dress, blouse, or skirt.

Pleat: A decorative feature on a garment in which fabric has been doubled over, pressed, and stitched in place.

Queue: A ponytail of hair gathered at the back of a wig with a band.

R

Ready-to-wear: Clothing manufactured in standard sizes and sold to customers without custom alterations.

S

Silhouette: The general shape or outline of the human body.

Single-breasted: A jacket fastened down the front with a single row of buttons. *See also* Double-breasted.

Sole: The bottom of a shoe, covering the bottom of the foot.

Straights: The forms, or lasts, used to make the soles of shoes without differentiating between the left and right feet.

Suede: Skin from a young goat, called kidskin or calfskin, buffed to a velvet-like finish.

Synthetic: A term used to describe chemically made fabrics, such as nylon, acrylic, polyester, and vinyl.

T

Taffeta: A shiny, smooth fabric woven of silk or other materials.

Textile: A cloth or fabric, especially when woven or knitted.

Throat: The opening of a shoe at the instep.

Twill: A fabric with a diagonal line pattern woven onto the surface.

U

Upper: The parts of a shoe above the sole.

V

Velvet: A fabric with a short, plush pile of silk, cotton, or other material.

 W

Wig: A head covering worn to conceal the hair or to cover a bald head.

Fashion, Costume, *and* Culture

Clothing, Headwear, Body Decorations, and Footwear through the Ages

Europe in the Fifteenth Century

Europe at the dawn of the fifteenth century operated much as it had for the previous several hundred years. The majority of the people, known as peasants, worked on small farms and paid some form of tax to a local lord, who provided the land on which they worked and also offered protection. These lords, who might be dukes, barons, or even kings, were the leading figures in the various kingdoms, states, duchys (the territory ruled by a duke), and other small regions by which most of Europe was organized. They were surrounded by advisers and leading merchants, who formed their court, and also by warriors, known as knights, who fought for them. In some parts of Europe, especially in England and France, these lords began to ally themselves behind the power of one king. (Henry VII united England during his reign, from 1485 to 1509, and Francis I later did the same for France during his reign from 1515 to 1547.) These alliances of nobles under one king began the process that eventually organized Europe into the nations we know today. But at the dawn of the fifteenth century this process had just begun, and for the most part the political organization of Europe was characterized by distinct and often warring kingdoms.

Though the many kingdoms of Europe often vied for power with each other, sometimes fighting bloody and destructive wars, they were united in several important ways. First, they all fell under the authority of the Catholic Church, which up until the

Europeans in the fifteenth century typically wore clothing rich in colors and fabrics. *Reproduced by permission of © Archivo Iconografico, S.A./CORBIS.*

sixteenth century was the sole religious institution in all of Europe. Europeans were also connected by growing networks of trade and commerce. Roads established during the Roman Empire (27 B.C.E.–476 C.E.) linked European kingdoms and helped them move goods from kingdom to kingdom. Finally, they were also linked in their clothing styles. Though there were some important regional variations, for the most part people in England, France, Italy, Germany, and Spain tended to dress similarly.

A Renaissance of learning and culture

Beginning in the late fourteenth century and escalating in the fifteenth century, two regions began to lead a rebirth, called the Renaissance, of learning, culture, and commerce. This Renaissance began in Italy, especially around the city of Florence, and in a region known as Burgundy, which included parts of modern-day France and Holland. The Italian states developed banking and trading systems that helped stabilize the economy throughout Europe. The duchy of Burgundy also grew very wealthy. In both areas wealthy nobles and merchants poured money into art, learning, clothing, and decoration such as jewelry. The Renaissance is known for its abundance of fine art and architecture, and for its renewed emphasis on literature and learning. But it also encouraged merchants and traders to expand their businesses. Soon these businesspeople extended their trade further and further. One of the most thriving industries in early Europe was the textile industry, which made rich fabrics available to more people than ever before. Soon the Renaissance spread to the rest of Europe.

By the middle of the fifteenth century, Europe was ready for the Renaissance that had begun in Italy and Burgundy. The end of the Hundred Years' War (1337–1453) between France and England allowed those two emerging nations to concentrate their energies on internal issues rather than war. After 1469 the kingdom of Spain grew more stable, as did the nearby kingdom of Portugal. Though Germany was divided into a number of smaller states, these too were fairly stable. The increased stability in these nations allowed people to concentrate on developing trade and commerce, which in turn created wealth for a larger number of people. This growing interest in trade also fed directly into the rise of exploration that saw European explorers, especially from Spain, Portugal, and England, discovering new territories and trade routes around the world. All of these trends combined to create the cultural flowering during the late fifteenth century known as the Renaissance.

The fifteenth century was a great era of transition in Europe, and that transition was also seen in the clothing worn by Europeans.

FOR MORE INFORMATION

Johnson, Paul. *The Renaissance: A Short History.* New York: Modern Library, 2000.

Kallen, Stuart A. *The 1400s.* San Diego, CA: Greenhaven Press, 2001.

Langley, Andrew. *Renaissance.* New York: Knopf, 1999.

Thompson, Stephen P., ed. *The Renaissance.* San Diego, CA: Greenhaven Press, 2000.

Fifteenth-Century Clothing

The fifteenth century saw transformations in the nature of costume and culture that are key to our understanding of Western fashion. Up until the fifteenth century, the clothing customs of most cultures had been determined by tradition, the availability of certain kinds of fabric, and the skill of the tailor. Ancient Egyptians wore similar clothing for nearly thirty centuries, for example, and the long wool garments worn by Europeans in the sixth century were not that different from those worn in the fourteenth century.

Various styles of fifteenth-century costume, including women's long, flowing gowns and men's hose and breeches. *Reproduced by permission of © Bettmann/ CORBIS.*

During the fifteenth century, however, the nature of European costume began to emphasize fashion, the current style or custom of dress.

In the late Middle Ages (c. 500–c. 1500), only the wealthiest members of a royal court had the resources to regularly change their costume and accessories. But during the early years of the Renaissance, or cultural rebirth, which started in the fifteenth century, more and more people began to acquire the wealth that allowed them to dress more extravagantly and keep up with the newly popular styles. In Burgundy, a kingdom in present-day France, and in Italian states such as Florence, greater numbers of wealthy merchants, nobles, and others competed to wear the most striking and elegant clothes. Certain people, such as Philip III (1396–1467), duke of Burgundy, who ruled from 1419 to 1467, became trendsetters, people who introduced a fashion that others followed. The clothing styles and customs that were introduced in Italy and Burgundy began to spread and by the end of the century, the emphasis on fashion and the wealth that was required to pursue fashion had stretched throughout Europe.

Costume of the early fifteenth century

The clothing of the early fifteenth century continued the traditions from the late Middle Ages. Both men and women continued to wear the houppelande, a long gown that covered the body from the neck to the floor. Houppelandes were made in a variety of fabrics, from simple wool to rich silk and velvet. Women's houppelandes were increasingly tailored so that the gown fit closely across the upper body, while the skirt billowed outward. Women also wore the bliaut, another long gown. Increasingly men choose to wear hose and breeches on their legs, and a tunic or a pourpoint (a closely fitted, padded overshirt) on their upper body. The pourpoint evolved in the fifteenth century into the doublet, the most common male garment of the century. Both men and women also wore a variety of overgarments, including a light cape called a mantle, and the cote and cotehardie, similar to the ones worn in the Middle Ages.

The costume revolution of the late fifteenth century

Several important trends came together in the late fifteenth century to mark a real change in costume styles across Europe. The first, mentioned earlier, was the general rise in wealth across the continent. Increased political stability and expanding trade meant that more people in the growing European cities could afford the finer things in life, notably clothing. The growing wealth allowed people to wear a variety of different fabrics, including silk, taffeta, and velvet, along with the traditional cotton, wool, and linen. Some of the wealthiest industries in early Europe grew out of the production of textiles, or fabrics.

This general increase in wealth allowed the tastes and preferences of the wealthy in Italy and Burgundy to spread across Europe. Following these trends, men wore more closely fitting hose and doublets. Their doublets, which had once been buttoned to the neck, opened to an ever-deeper V neck, with long laces crossing the V and revealing a shirt beneath, usually made of white linen. Men's hose were sewn together at the genital area, and we see the first use of the codpiece, a padded covering for the genitals. At the end of the century, padding in men's clothes created the appearance of broad shoulders.

Women's clothing also saw changes late in the century. Gone was the bunching of fabric in front of the stomach, which had created a pregnant look, and the billowing sleeves. Women's gowns became much more closely fitted in the torso and arms, while skirts billowed outward. Beginning in 1468 women in Spain began to use round hoops worn inside their skirts to give the skirt shape and make it swish when they walked. These hoops, called farthingales, would be very popular in the sixteenth century.

Increasing wealth and a desire on the part of people to use dress as a marker of status led to the relatively swift changes in clothing styles that we know today as fashion. In fact, one of the first fashion crazes began in 1477 when Swiss soldiers introduced a trend called slashing, in which small cuts were made in an outer garment to reveal the rich fabric beneath. Soon this style was copied throughout Europe and used on all varieties of garments.

The trends that began in the fifteenth century truly became widespread in the sixteenth century, when all of Europe flowered during the period known as the Renaissance.

FOR MORE INFORMATION

Annenburg/CPB. *What Was It Like to Really Live in the Middle Ages?: Clothing.* http://www.learner.org/exhibits/middleages/clothing.html (accessed on August 6, 2003).

Batterberry, Michael, and Ariane Batterberry. *Fashion: The Mirror of History.* New York: Greenwich House, 1977.

Cosgrave, Bronwyn. *The Complete History of Costume and Fashion: From Ancient Egypt to the Present Day.* New York: Checkmark Books, 2000.

Laver, James. *Costume and Fashion: A Concise History.* 4th ed. London, England: Thames and Hudson, 2002.

Payne, Blanche, Geitel Winakor, and Jane Farrell-Beck. *The History of Costume.* 2nd ed. New York: HarperCollins, 1992.

Dagging and Slashing

Seen between the late fourteenth and sixteenth centuries, dagging and slashing were decorative techniques that were used to distinguish and beautify garments. Both techniques were used on the common garments of the day to add decoration in accordance with fashion trends. In this way they were related to similar fashion trends throughout human history, such as the use of clavi, or stripes, on Roman togas and tunicas or the use of fringe on shirts in the twentieth century. Both dagging and slashing illustrated the growing importance of intricate, unique details in fashion in the Renaissance.

Dagging involved cutting a series of patterns in the edges of fabric. Those patterns, or dagges, could be long U or V shapes, or complex leaf-like designs. Beginning in the fourteenth century and proceeding well into the fifteenth century, dagges were cut into the edges of sleeves and hems of both men's and women's garments, including houppelandes, bliauts, cotes (all long gowns and robes), and virtually any outer garment.

The decorative technique known as slashing involved making small cuts in the outer fabric of a garment so as to reveal the inner lining. As with dagging, slashing was

Dagging, seen here on this man's sleeves, is a decorative edge that was commonly used to distinguish and beautify the clothing of fifteenth-century Europeans. *Courtesy of the Library of Congress.*

performed on all variety of garments, from men's doublets, a padded overshirt, and breeches to women's gowns and even to shoes. The practice of slashing was introduced by Swiss army troops following their defeat of Charles the Bold (1433–1477), duke of Burgundy, in 1477. As the tattered Swiss troops ransacked the villages of Burgundy, a region of present-day France, they cut up bits of tents and banners and threaded these scraps through holes in their own garments. The effect was to have brightly colored pieces of fabric poking out from underneath an outer garment. Upon their return home, wealthy people began to imitate the fashion and it soon caught on throughout Europe. Slashing remained popular in Europe through the 1500s.

FOR MORE INFORMATION

Cosgrave, Bronwyn. *The Complete History of Costume and Fashion: From Ancient Egypt to the Present Day.* New York: Checkmark Books, 2000.

Laver, James. *Costume and Fashion: A Concise History.* 4th ed. London, England: Thames and Hudson, 2002.

Payne, Blanche, Geitel Winakor, and Jane Farrell-Beck. *The History of Costume.* 2nd ed. New York: HarperCollins, 1992.

Doublet

The doublet, a slightly padded short overshirt, usually buttoned down the front, with or without sleeves, was one of the essential men's garments of the fifteenth and sixteenth centuries. The basic form of the doublet came from the pourpoint, a padded shirt that was originally worn by knights under their armor. This form-fitting shirt was soon worn by most upper-class men. While the basic shape of the doublet remained the same, the garment was modified in many ways over the course of the several centuries in which it was worn, thus keeping it in fashion.

The name doublet referred to the duplicate layers of material used to make the shirt. The inner lining was usually made of linen, while the outer layer was made of heavy silk. Depending on the current fashion, these layers were filled with various amounts

The doublet, a slightly padded overshirt as seen in this illustration, was one of the essential men's garments of the fifteenth and sixteenth centuries.
Reproduced by permission of © Historical Picture Archive/ CORBIS.

of bombast, or padding. During the late fifteenth and early sixteenth century padding was added to the shoulders and upper arms, making the shoulders look very broad. One fashion of the late sixteenth century was called a peascod-belly, which made the lower stomach area so filled with padding that it made a man look pregnant. The doublet usually ended right at the waist and sometimes came to a point in the front. It was worn at first with a short skirt and later with breeches, a type of pants, and hose.

The doublet was a key garment in the transition from the long, draped garments of the Middle Ages to the more fitted styles of the Renaissance. At first the doublet was buttoned all the way to the neck, but during the late fifteenth century the neckline of the doublet opened to a wide V shape, the better to show off the linen shirts and ruffs, or pleated collars, that were becoming fashionable. The sleeves showed changes, varying from tightly fitting from shoulder to wrist, to very puffy at the upper arms. Often sleeves were separate garments that were fastened at the shoulder, with the fasteners hidden by small wings on the doublet. Beginning in the late fifteenth century, doublets were one of the primary garments to use slashing, a fashion statement that involved making small slits in the outer fabric of the doublet and then pulling out or revealing pieces of the inner lining.

FOR MORE INFORMATION

Laver, James. *Costume and Fashion: A Concise History.* 4th ed. London, England: Thames and Hudson, 2002.

Payne, Blanche, Geitel Winakor, and Jane Farrell-Beck. *The History of Costume.* 2nd ed. New York: HarperCollins, 1992.

Yarwood, Doreen. *The Encyclopedia of World Costume.* New York: Charles Scribner's Sons, 1978.

[*See also* **Volume 2, Europe in the Middle Ages: Pourpoint; Volume 3, Fifteenth Century: Dagging and Slashing; Volume 3, Sixteenth Century: Sleeves**]

Fifteenth-Century Headwear

Like many of the fashion trends of the fifteenth century, the headwear worn during the fifteenth century underwent a shift after about the 1470s. In the first part of the century, headwear and hairstyles generally followed the conventions of the late Middle Ages (c. 500–c. 1500). Men tended to wear their hair in a bowl cut, although Italian men tended to prefer longer, curlier hair. Men were generally clean shaven. In fact, an English law from 1447 made it a crime for a man to grow a mustache. Men could wear a variety of hats, from the common hood, a staple of the Middle Ages, to the turban and a wide variety of other hats. One of the more popular hats of the early fifteenth century was the sugar-loaf hat, a felt or wool hat that was worn close to the head at the top and back and had a large bulge, shaped like an oval loaf of sugar (sugar was packaged at the time in these large loaves), sticking off the back top of the head.

Women's hair was obscured in most tapestries and paintings of the period, following the custom of having married women cover their hair. Before marriage, however, women wore their hair very long, often braided and piled on top of the head. For wealthy women, the headdress was an essential part of the wardrobe. Much time and energy was spent plucking or shaving hair from the forehead and the back of the neck to keep hair from appearing from below the rim of the elaborate hats that were worn. Along with the steeple and ram's horn headdresses of the fourteenth century, women added a variety of headwear that towered over or elongated the profile of the head. Decorative veils were hung from various parts of the headwear, not for modesty but to add decoration and bulk. Many women used a bourrelet, a thick padded roll, to add bulk to their headwear. The bourrelet could be worn at the top or the back of the head and was held in place with straps or pins. This heavy headwear was most likely very uncomfortable and surely

Hats were an extremely popular piece of headwear for men in the fifteenth century. *Reproduced by permission of © Adam Woolfitt/ CORBIS.*

restricted movement. Both men and women of the lower classes continued to wear simpler headwear such as a coif, a small cloth tied around the head beneath the chin, or a simple beret. Out of modesty, women covered their necks with a wimple or a barbe, simple pieces of fabric that covered the chin and neck.

Later in the fifteenth century men's hairstyles began to show some real changes. Perhaps following the conventions of Italian men—among the richest and best-dressed in all of Europe—men throughout Europe began to wear their hair longer, sometimes to shoulder length. Men generally did not wear beards and mustaches, but facial hair did become popular for brief periods of time in each of the European states. Hat styles remained similar, though more ornament was added. Feathers especially became popular late in the century.

Women continued to wear tall, cone-shaped headdresses into the 1480s and to raise their foreheads by shaving and plucking. After the 1480s, however, the tall projections disappeared from headwear, replaced by much smaller headdresses that framed the face. These fabric headdresses might be richly adorned with jewels or embroidery. As headwear styles grew simpler, hairstyles grew more complex. Hair was braided and woven into ornate buns and decorated with ribbons, jewels, and strings of pearls. False hair was used to add to a hairstyle, and many of the richest women wore wigs to avoid having to spend so much time having their hair styled. Hair dying was most common in Italy, where blonde was the favorite color, as it had been since the time of the Roman Republic (509–27 B.C.E.).

FOR MORE INFORMATION

Corson, Richard. *Fashions in Hair: The First Five Thousand Years.* London, England: Peter Owen, 2001.

Cosgrave, Bronwyn. *The Complete History of Costume and Fashion: From Ancient Egypt to the Present Day.* New York: Checkmark Books, 2000.

Payne, Blanche, Geitel Winakor, and Jane Farrell-Beck. *The History of Costume.* 2nd ed. New York: HarperCollins, 1992.

Barbe

During the late Middle Ages (c. 500–c. 1500) and early Renaissance, a married woman was generally not considered properly dressed without a head covering of some sort. There were many types of head coverings and other accessories that covered not only a woman's head and hair, but also modestly draped her ears and neck so that only her face was visible. One of these accessories, which was popular during the 1300s and early 1400s, was the barbe, a more formal version of the wimple, another form of neck drapery. Named after the French word for "beard," the barbe was a piece of cloth that fit directly under a woman's chin and hung down to cover her chest, somewhat like a man's beard. Most barbes were made of simple white linen fabric, and many were pleated with tiny folds ironed into the cloth. The sides of the barbe were brought up on either side of the head, covering the ears, and pinned on top of the head. A veil or other head covering was usually worn with the barbe.

A variation of the barbe was the simpler barbette, or "little beard." The barbette was a strip of linen fabric, which passed under the chin, over the ears, and around the top of the head. The barbette did not provide quite as much coverage as the barbe but was a very common part of women's headgear. Barbes were very modest garments and were often worn by widows or other women in mourning.

FOR MORE INFORMATION

Laver, James. *Costume and Fashion: A Concise History.* New York: Thames and Hudson, 2002.

[*See also* **Volume 2, Europe in the Middle Ages: Wimple**]

Fifteenth-Century Body Decorations

The fifteenth century was a time of transition in the ways that people ornamented their bodies. The use of jewelry and accessories became more and more prevalent and showy over the course of the century, reflecting the growing richness of the various kingdoms of Europe and paving the way for the absolute excess of display that occurred in the sixteenth century.

As in the early Middle Ages (c. 500–c. 1500), bathing was not a regular practice throughout most of Europe, except for in Italy. Wealthy people might bathe once every few weeks and the poorer classes bathed far less frequently. In order to mask what must have been very strong body odor, wealthy people used large amounts of perfume. Perfumes of the fifteenth century were fairly simple, consisting of crushed blends of natural products such as flowers and spices. (The extraction of oils to create modern perfumes did not occur until the sixteenth century.) Some people carried small metal balls called pomanders that were filled with crushed flowers or herbs; they waved these in front of their noses to mask offensive odors.

Makeup provided women with subtle ways of enhancing their appearance. The general trend during the fifteenth century was toward understated, discreet makeup, so women did not use bold colors for rouge or eye makeup. Instead they used a variety of treatments to make their skin appear pale and used subtle shades of pink to add blush to their cheeks or red to color their lips. Women continued to use white lead and other dangerous chemicals to whiten their face, unaware of the consequences to their skin and health. Because they didn't bathe very often, these toxic layers of white face paint might stay on for several days.

As the kingdoms of Europe became wealthier, members of the royal courts used jewelry to display their wealth. The wealthiest citizens of the city-states of Italy, especially Florence, and the kingdom of Burgundy, in present-day France, led the way in the use of jewelry. They hired expert craftsmen to make detailed gold jewelry, including necklaces, rings, and pendants. They also showed the first preference for diamonds, and jewelers developed new cutting techniques to show off the brilliance of this gem. The love of jewelry soon spread throughout Europe and certain forms of jewelry became especially popular. Necklaces and wide jeweled collars displayed precious gems or plaques and pendants of gold. Jewels were also added to the belts that were worn with most garments. These belts, some of which could be quite broad, might also be adorned with gold chains holding keys, a mirror, or a scented ball. The most popular form of jewelry was the ring. Rings could be worn on every finger and were custom made with detailed designs and many different jewels. Earrings were not common during the fifteenth century, except in Spain, where they became popular toward the end of the century.

Another important accessory of the period was a pair of gloves. The skills of tailors increased in the late fourteenth century, allowing for the creation of very finely fitted clothes of thin leather made from the skin of deer and rabbit. Gloves might have decorative fur cuffs and were often perfumed, partly to mask the smell of the leather.

FOR MORE INFORMATION

Batterberry, Michael, and Ariane Batterberry. *Fashion: The Mirror of History.* New York: Greenwich House, 1977.

Bigelow, Marybelle S. *Fashion in History: Apparel in the Western World.* Minneapolis, MN: Burgess Publishing, 1970.

Cosgrave, Bronwyn. *The Complete History of Costume and Fashion: From Ancient Egypt to the Present Day.* New York: Checkmark Books, 2000.

Irvine, Susan. *Perfume: The Creation and Allure of Classic Fragrances.* London, England: Arum Press, 1995.

Fifteenth-Century Footwear

Europeans wore a wide variety of footwear during the fifteenth century, from simple pull-on leather moccasins to highly decorated poulaines, extremely long, pointed shoes. Shoes were generally made of leather, with either wood or leather for soles. They might be held to the foot with laces or with buckles. Working people generally wore heavier leather shoes and boots, but the upper classes, who provide most of the information about clothing styles since they were the ones who often left the most records, wore fancier shoes.

There were also several different footwear styles that were popular for a time. For the early part of the fifteenth century the trend in footwear was to have pointy toes. Shoes of all styles tended to come to a point. The most popular footwear among nobles in the courts of the various kingdoms of Europe were the crackowes and the poulaines that had become so popular in the fourteenth century. These soft-soled leather shoes had very long points, some extending for nearly two feet, and often had decorative flaps and buckles. Competition to see who could wear the longest shoes made the points ever longer.

The trend toward pointy shoes came to an end around the 1470s, when a major shift in taste changed fashions throughout Europe. The long, lean look faded and was replaced by a preference for broad, chunky shapes. As a result, most shoes had blunt, squared-off toes. The most extreme examples had toe boxes, with the fronts of the shoe looking almost swollen.

Men continued to wear hose throughout the fifteenth century, and many of these hose covered the feet, with either a light leather sole or no sole at all. Historians have wondered how men kept these hose from getting dirty or wearing through. One way to protect the soles of hose was to wear pattens. Pattens were wooden overshoes that could be worn outdoors and usually had two wooden blocks that raised the foot above the mud and dust of the streets. Some form of patten has also been used in Japan and in Arab countries.

Women's shoes seemed to have followed the general trends of men's shoes, moving from long and pointy to short and rounded. The long dresses that women wore, however, hid their feet from view in most portraits and artifacts, preventing a detailed picture of their footwear.

FOR MORE INFORMATION

Cosgrave, Bronwyn. *The Complete History of Costume and Fashion: From Ancient Egypt to the Present Day.* New York: Checkmark Books, 2000.

Payne, Blanche, Geitel Winakor, and Jane Farrell-Beck. *The History of Costume.* 2nd ed. New York: HarperCollins, 1992.

[*See also* **Volume 2, Europe in the Middle Ages: Crackowes and Poulaines**]

The Sixteenth Century

The sixteenth century is widely considered to be one of the pivotal centuries in human history, a time when the overall organization and structure of human society went through a fundamental change. It was the high point of a larger historical period known as the Renaissance, which lasted from the late fourteenth through the sixteenth century. It was called the Renaissance because Europe saw a rebirth of learning, arts, and culture that had not been seen since the splendor of the Greek and Roman empires of a thousand years past. This rebirth was encouraged by the rise of universities, the creation of the first printing press in 1455, which allowed book publication to flourish, and widespread support for the arts by wealthy patrons. But more than a rebirth occurred in Europe in the sixteenth century. Expanding trade created wealth and new industries, helping to fuel the growth of the middle class; religious controversy sparked war and contributed to the growing strength and independence of nations throughout Europe; and the invention of new technologies revolutionized agriculture and industry, allowing for greater population growth. This key century is often thought to have begun the modern period of history, which continues to this day.

Perhaps the greatest trendsetter of the sixteenth century was the powerful Elizabeth I of England, who drove fashion to extremes in her pursuit of richness and ornament. *Reproduced by permission of SuperStock, Inc.*

Powerful nations

Perhaps the most significant political trend of the century was the consolidation of power in the hands of monarchs ruling large kingdoms, or nations. During the Middle Ages (c. 500–c. 1500) many minor kings, dukes, and other nobles had governed small regions. They engaged in frequent, disruptive wars with each other. By the sixteenth century, however, nobles in the regions that became England, France, and Spain had come up with a system that promoted greater stability. They gave their support—in the form of taxes and soldiers—to a single powerful monarch. The unifying presence of a stable monarch ruling over a large area reduced the threat of frequent warfare and allowed trade to expand in the areas under the monarch's rule. The economies of France, England, and Spain improved as a result, helped along by the opening of trade routes in the New World in the Western Hemisphere. The monarch's power rested on the confidence that was entrusted in him or her by the country's many nobles, so it was not always stable.

Not all of the areas of Europe were so unified and organized. In what is now Italy, city-states were the primary form of organization, and they were controlled by wealthy families who were some of the leading figures of the Renaissance, such as the Medici family. These city-states thrived on banking and trade. In present-day Germany a variety of states were loosely organized under the authority of the pope. Both of these regions would not organize into unified nations until the nineteenth century.

The Protestant Reformation

One of the forces that had united Europe throughout the Middle Ages was the religious unity provided by the Roman Catholic Church. That unity crumbled in the fifteenth and especially the sixteenth century, and this collapse actually contributed to the strength of the monarchies. The most powerful force behind the decline of the Catholic Church was a historical event called the Protestant Reformation. The Reformation began in 1517 when German priest Martin Luther (1483–1546) posted a series of protests about church abuses on the door of a local Catholic church. Soon many others joined Luther in his break from Catholicism. By the end of the century these protesting groups, called Protestants, had created distinct religions of their own. These new religions, such as Lutheranism, Calvinism, and Puritanism, became especially influential in northern Europe.

With Protestants set against Catholics, and with Catholics in different parts of Europe arguing over divisions of power, religion became a source of real conflict throughout Europe. Powerful monarchs, such as Henry VIII of England (1491–1547), decided that they, not the pope, should be the head of the church in their nation. In 1534 Henry VIII declared himself the head of the Church of England. The overall decline in authority of the Catholic Church led to an increase in the authority of the ruling monarchies.

There were many, many more important events and trends that shaped the sixteenth century, not least the further opening of the New World to trade and exploration, but the rise of powerful nations with strong and complex economies had the greatest impact on the course of human costume.

FOR MORE INFORMATION

Corrick, James A. *The Renaissance*. San Diego, CA: Lucent Books, 1998.

The European Emergence: Timeframe A.D. 1500–1600. Alexandria, VA: Time-Life Books, 1989.

Johnson, Paul. *The Renaissance: A Short History*. New York: Modern Library, 2000.

Renaissance. 10 vols. Danbury, CT: Grolier Educational, 2002.

Shuter, Jane. *The Renaissance*. Chicago, IL: Heinemann Library, 2000.

Sixteenth-Century Clothing

The sixteenth century was one of the most extravagant and splendid periods in all of costume history and one of the first periods in which modern ideas of fashion influenced what people wore. Some of the larger cultural trends of the time included the rise and spread of books, the expansion of trade and exploration, and the increase in power and wealth of national monarchies, or kingdoms, in France, England, and Spain. Each of these trends influenced what people chose to wear and contributed to the frequent changes in style and the emergence of style trendsetters that are characteristic of modern fashion.

Wealth and the monarchies of Europe

Perhaps the single biggest factor influencing fashion in the sixteenth century was the wealth of European kingdoms and powerful city-states in Italy. Trade and exploration had led to a boom in the economies of Europe, and the textile, or fabric, industries were at the center of that boom. Wool production in England and silk production in Italy were especially important. These industries allowed for the creation of rich fabrics. At the same time tailors guilds, or associations of craftsmen, proved very skilled at turning these fabrics into luxurious clothes. The monarchs and the members of their court were enriched by these trends and could afford the most expensive clothes. But the guild members, traders, and merchants who made up a growing middle class could also afford these clothes.

The powerful kings and queens who led European nations believed that one of the ways that they could display their power was through their clothing. Powerful leaders had always set an example by their clothes, but King Francis I of France (1494–1547), who ruled from 1515 to 1547, was the first to become a true fashion

The family of Emperor Maximilian I wearing layers of rich, ornate clothing and jewelry. The powerful kings and queens who led European nations believed one of the ways they could display their power was through their dress. *Reproduced by permission of © Archivo Iconografico, S.A./CORBIS.*

trendsetter. He deliberately and carefully chose unique and outlandish outfits, and then challenged members of the royal court to adopt his styles as a way of asserting his leadership. Other monarchs followed Francis's lead. French King Henry III, who ruled from 1574 to 1589, set new standards for French luxury and popularized the use of lace for men, though his critics said that he dressed too much like a woman. Perhaps the greatest fashion trendsetter of the century was Elizabeth I of England, who ruled from 1558 to 1603. This pow-

erful female ruler drove fashion to extremes in her pursuit of richness and ornament. Upon her death she was said to have collected three thousand gowns, eighty wigs, and an abundance of jewelry.

Fashion historian Ruth M. Green commented in the introduction to Jack Cassin-Scott's *Costume and Fashion in Colour, 1550–1760,* "fashion was initiated in courts and spread from them like ripples in a pond." Merchants and members of the middle class followed the lead of the court, and poorer members of society even tried to find ways to imitate the styles of those above them in the social order. The poorest people could scarcely copy the fashions of the wealthy, but they did change the form of their garments to follow trends and could sometimes gain access to discarded or secondhand garments.

The pressure to keep up

People's attempts to stay in fashion could be very costly. In England and France large owners of land were expected to entertain the monarch and their court when they traveled about the country. They felt pressured to throw large parties and to clothe themselves and their families in the latest and most expensive fashions. When the royal courts traveled, they nearly made the outlying nobles go broke trying to keep up with their standard of display. As Michael and Ariane Batterberry wrote in *Fashion: The Mirror of History,* "At the great country houses the 'progresses' of the queen and her entourage were as welcome as a visitation from assassins."

Monarchs and nobles weren't the only ones giving fashion guidance during the sixteenth century. People began to use new printed books to get information about clothing and manners. The first book of fashion advice for men was Count Baldassare Castiglione's *Il Cortegiano* (1561), which was translated into several languages, including English as *The Book of the Courtier.* Along with advice on conversation, horse riding, and other manners, Castiglione urged men to develop their own sense of style. Similar books soon became available for women.

Basic garments of the century

For all the changes that fashion brought to the clothing of the sixteenth century, the basic form of garments remained fairly stable.

The standard garments worn by men were hose and breeches for the lower body and a doublet, a padded overshirt, with attached sleeves for the upper body. During the early part of the century men often wore a prominent codpiece over their genitals, but this garment virtually disappeared by the end of the century. Both men and women wore ruffs, wide pleated collars, around their necks. Men wore a shirt beneath their doublets, and they wore a variety of cloaks and mantles, a type of cape, over the doublet. Perhaps the most memorable was the mandilion, a cloak draped over one shoulder almost purely as a fashion statement. The basic garment for women was the gown, but it was far from simple. Actually a combination of several garments, including bodice, sleeves, skirts, and underskirts, sixteenth-century gowns have been considered some of the most beautiful garments of any era in history.

The fact that certain garments were worn consistently throughout the century does not mean those garments stayed the same. The cut, color, and finish of garments changed considerably in response to fashion. People used embroidery, jewels, lace, ribbons, and many other forms of decoration to continually seek ways to express their own sense of style.

FOR MORE INFORMATION

Batterberry, Michael, and Ariane Batterberry. *Fashion: The Mirror of History*. New York: Greenwich House, 1977.

Cassin-Scott, Jack. *Costume and Fashion in Colour, 1550–1760*. Introduction by Ruth M. Green. Dorset, England: Blandford Press, 1975.

Cosgrave, Bronwyn. *The Complete History of Costume and Fashion: From Ancient Egypt to the Present Day*. New York: Checkmark Books, 2000.

Jones, Ann Rosalind, and Peter Stallybrass. *Renaissance Clothing and the Materials of Memory*. New York: Cambridge University Press, 2000.

LaMar, Virginia A. *English Dress in the Age of Shakespeare*. Washington, DC: Folger Shakespeare Library, 1958.

Laver, James. *Costume and Fashion: A Concise History*. 4th ed. London, England: Thames and Hudson, 2002.

"Overview of an Elizabethan Outfit." *The Elizabethan Costuming Page.* http://www.costume.dm.net/overview.html (accessed on August 6, 2003).

Payne, Blanche, Geitel Winakor, and Jane Farrell-Beck. *The History of Costume*. 2nd ed. New York: HarperCollins, 1992.

Bases

Bases were a form of skirt, worn by upper-class members of the military, that were a striking departure from typical men's costume of the sixteenth century. During this period, most men wore a doublet, a slightly padded short overshirt, with hose and breeches. The bases replaced the hose and breeches. They were made of stiff, heavy cloth, and consisted of panels of fabric, often in alternating colors. The panels were attached to an inner lining in such a way as to make each of the panels either rounded or pleated. These skirts were worn for ceremonial purposes throughout Europe, especially for the large military reviews that allowed European armies to show off their strength. Men typically wore form-fitting leg stockings beneath the bases.

Bases were a form of skirt, made of heavy panels of fabric, worn by upper-class members of the military. *Reproduced by permission of © Art & Immagini srl/CORBIS.*

FOR MORE INFORMATION

Payne, Blanche, Geitel Winakor, and Jane Farrell-Beck. *The History of Costume.* 2nd ed. New York: HarperCollins, 1992.

Bombast

Bombast was absolutely essential to the men's and women's clothing of the sixteenth century, yet it was never actually seen. Bombast was a form of stuffing made from cotton, wool, horsehair, or even sawdust. It was used to pad and add shape to a variety of garments, including the shoulders, chest, and stomach of the doublet, a kind of overshirt, and bodice; the bulky legs of men's hose like pumpkin breeches and Venetians; or the sleeves and shoulders of women's gowns. These garments could not have attained their exaggerated shape without the use of bombast. Today, the word "bombast" is used to refer to exaggerated speech or writing, and someone who uses such speech is referred to as "bombastic."

FOR MORE INFORMATION

Bigelow, Marybelle S. *Fashion in History: Apparel in the Western World.* Minneapolis, MN: Burgess Publishing, 1970.

Payne, Blanche, Geitel Winakor, and Jane Farrell-Beck. *The History of Costume.* 2nd ed. New York: HarperCollins, 1992.

[*See also* **Volume 3, Fifteenth Century: Doublet; Volume 3, Sixteenth Century: Hose and Breeches; Volume 3, Seventeenth Century: Gowns**]

Codpiece

During the fourteenth, fifteenth, and sixteenth centuries, the most common everyday clothing for men was a kind of short jacket or overshirt called a doublet worn with thick woolen, linen, or silk hose. The hosiery of the time consisted of two separate stockings that covered the legs but left an opening at the top that exposed the wearer's genitals. To preserve modesty and protect the genitals, medieval tailors invented the codpiece around the mid-1400s. The codpiece, called a *braguette* in French, was a flap or pouch of fabric sewn at the top of a man's hose to hide his genitals from view.

While the codpiece was originally created to provide modesty, it evolved into a fashion statement. By the early 1500s, the codpiece had grown larger and more decorative and had become a way to advertise one's masculinity, by exaggerating the size of his genitals. Though doublets became long enough to cover the genitals, most had a special opening in the front for the codpiece to stick through in a visible way. Some codpieces were even designed to curve upward to resemble an erect penis. Fashionable men, led by England's King Henry VIII (1491–1547), padded their codpieces to enormous sizes and decorated them with jewels. Some even used them as a sort of pocket, hiding small weapons or valuables there.

Priests and other clergy were horrified by the new style and spoke out against it. The codpiece did indeed get smaller by the mid-1500s, possibly because Queen Elizabeth I (1533–1603) was the new ruler of England and did not appreciate this example of male vanity. By 1575 the codpiece had disappeared, replaced by short padded breeches, or pants, which provided coverage.

FOR MORE INFORMATION

All the Rage. Alexandria, VA: Time-Life Books, 1992.

Called a *braguette* in French, the codpiece was a flap or pouch of fabric sewn at the top of a man's hose. *Reproduced by permission of © Archivo Iconografico, S.A./ CORBIS.*

Bigelow, Marybelle S. *Fashion in History: Apparel in the Western World.* Minneapolis, MN: Burgess Publishing, 1970.

Sichel, Marion. *History of Men's Costume.* London, England: Batsford, 1984.

Farthingales

Though farthingales were rarely seen, they were the item most responsible for the various distinctive shapes of women's skirts in the sixteenth century and beyond. A farthingale was a series of stiff hoops, usually made of wood or wicker, sewn into a fabric underskirt. It was anchored to the waist with ties and worn beneath a skirt to give the outer skirt a distinct shape.

The first farthingales were worn in Spain in about 1470 and were called vertugados. They had a small hoop just below the waist, with ever larger hoops further down the skirt. These hoops gave the skirt a perfect cone shape and allowed the outer skirt to drape in a smooth manner. As these farthingales became popular in France and England they became known as the Spanish farthingale. Many women in France and England wore two skirts over their farthingale, with the outermost skirt parted in front to reveal the contrasting middle skirt.

Later in the sixteenth century women began to experiment with widening the tops of their skirt profile. At first they added a padded roll around their waist, but later they adjusted the shape of the farthingale. One type of farthingale, called a French, wheel, or drum farthingale, used a series of identically round interior hoops. These gave the farthingale a cylindrical or drum shape. The outer skirt fit closely at the waist and then spread out over the farthingale in a cascade of folds. Finally, a bell farthingale used a combination of padding and hoops to give the skirts a large bell-shaped profile.

Though farthingales faded from widespread use by about the mid-seventeenth century, other forms of structures to give shape to skirts evolved over time including panniers, crinolines, and bustles.

FOR MORE INFORMATION

Bigelow, Marybelle S. *Fashion in History: Apparel in the Western World.* Minneapolis, MN: Burgess Publishing, 1970.

Cassin-Scott, Jack. *Costume and Fashion in Colour, 1550–1760.* Introduction by Ruth M. Green. Dorset, England: Blandford Press, 1975.

LaMar, Virginia A. *English Dress in the Age of Shakespeare.* Washington, DC: Folger Shakespeare Library, 1958.

Payne, Blanche, Geitel Winakor, and Jane Farrell-Beck. *The History of Costume.* 2nd ed. New York: HarperCollins, 1992.

Gowns

The only appropriate outfit for a well-bred woman of the sixteenth century was a complex ensemble that is known by the simple terms "gown," or "dress." These gowns, depicted in great detail in the many surviving paintings from the period, reveal the riches available to the members of the courts that surrounded European royalty. They could be constructed of luxurious materials like silk, velvet, and lace; lavishly adorned with pearls, beads, and jewels; and decorated with the most intricate patterns of stitching and embroidery. Those gowns worn by members of royalty and wealthy noblewomen were truly works of art. Even common women dressed in gowns that mimicked the wealthy in form, though not in the quality of the materials.

The lavish gowns worn by women from this period were made from at least three distinct parts: a bodice, a skirt, and sleeves. The bodice covered the torso and was similar to a man's doublet, the tight fitting double-layered garment that covered the body from shoulders to waist. The neckline opening of the bodice could vary widely in size, though the most common style was to have a large opening that revealed much of the shoulders and crossed the chest in a slight upward curve just above the breasts. By the end of the century necklines had grown very daring, revealing a woman's cleavage. Most often, however, the area above the neckline was filled with a chemise, a light, sometimes transparent shirt that rose to the neck and that very often ended in an attached and highly decorative ruff, a wide

APRONS AND SAFEGUARDS

Aprons and safeguards were two garments women used to protect their elaborate gowns. An apron was a panel of fabric worn at the front of a skirt, while a safeguard was a full outer skirt meant to protect the wearer from the weather. The garments were endlessly flexible in their form and their quality, allowing them to be worn by all classes of women.

For the poorest women, who might only have one nice skirt, an apron was worn to protect the skirts while working. A crude apron might be made of plain wool or cotton. Wealthy women wore aprons more for decoration than for protection. Their aprons could be made of luxurious fabrics like silk or velvet, and their patterns were chosen to complement the skirt. Fancy aprons were trimmed out in decorative lace and might be embroidered with intricate patterns. Aprons attached at the waist with a tie.

Safeguards were generally worn by wealthy women seeking to protect their expensive gowns. While these outer skirts were worn for protection, a stylish woman would have her safeguard made to match her outfit.

pleated collar. The front of the bodice was a V-shaped panel that came to a defined point at or below the waist. This triangular panel, called a stomacher, was often stiffened with bone or wood and padded with bombast in order to create a flat-chested appearance.

Attached to the bottom edge of the bodice was the skirt. While the bodice was intended to give the woman a slim silhouette, the skirts worn in the sixteenth century were very wide and full and reached all the way to the floor. Skirts were made of overlapping panels and used yards and yards of fabric. They were given their distinctive shape by farthingales, rigid hoops made of cane, bone, or wood. Stitched to the interior fabric of the skirt and anchored at the waist, these farthingales could give the skirts a distinct cone shape, as with the Spanish farthingale, or a drum or wheel shape. Some gowns had a wide opening at the front of the skirt that revealed either a separate underskirt or an interior panel of a different fabric, called a partlet. Women might also wear a decorative apron at the front of the skirt or a safeguard to protect the skirt when the woman was outdoors.

The final component of the gown was the sleeves. Some bodices had attached sleeves, but many sleeves were made separately and were attached to the bodice at the shoulders by means of points, or small ties. Sleeves varied tremendously in style, from formfitting to quite puffy, from a simple single fabric to intricate panels of several fabrics with lace, ribbons, and bows. Most sleeve styles combined some form of puff, often at the shoulder, with sections of more closely fitted fabric. Sleeves usually ended in an ornamental cuff. Many women also wore false sleeves, which hung at the sides of the dress.

Gown styles varied slightly from country to country, with Germans preferring a high-waisted look and Spanish women preferring a cone-shaped skirt, but all grew more ornate as the century progressed. Queen Elizabeth I of England, who ruled from 1558 to 1603, was known for her fantastically lavish gowns, and she set the style for all of Europe. At her death she was said to have possessed over three thousand different gowns.

FOR MORE INFORMATION

Cassin-Scott, Jack. *Costume and Fashion in Colour, 1550–1760.* Introduction by Ruth M. Green. Dorset, England: Blandford Press, 1975.

Cosgrave, Bronwyn. *The Complete History of Costume and Fashion: From Ancient Egypt to the Present Day.* New York: Checkmark Books, 2000.

LaMar, Virginia A. *English Dress in the Age of Shakespeare.* Washington, DC: Folger Shakespeare Library, 1958.

Payne, Blanche, Geitel Winakor, and Jane Farrell-Beck. *The History of Costume.* 2nd ed. New York: HarperCollins, 1992.

[*See also* Volume 3, Fifteenth Century: Doublet; Volume 3, Sixteenth Century: Bombast; Volume 3, Sixteenth Century: Farthingales; Volume 3, Sixteenth Century: Ruffs; Volume 3, Sixteenth Century: Sleeves; Volume 3, Seventeenth Century: Gowns]

For the poorest women, who might have only one nice skirt, an apron was worn to protect their clothing while working. *Reproduced by permission of © Gianni Dagli Orti/CORBIS.*

Hose and Breeches

Men in the sixteenth century had a number of choices about what to wear on their lower body, almost all involving some combination of breeches, or baggy pants, and hose. The basic combination of hose for the lower legs and breeches for the waist and upper legs had been in use since about 1200.

The simplest part of the hose and breeches combination was the hose, a precursor to knit stockings. Hose were made from a loosely woven fabric and they were cut on the bias, or diagonally, which allowed them to fit the legs snugly. It was very fashionable to show off the shape of the legs, and upper-class men sought out tailors skilled in making tight-fitting hose. Late in the century knitting began to be used to make hose, which made for a stretchy, formfitting look, but did not become common until the seventeenth century. If worn with longer breeches, hose might reach just to the knee and be held in place by a garter. By the fifteenth century, however, tailors had developed the ability to join what were once two

The man and boys are wearing hose and pumpkin breeches, which were often made in panels of alternating fabric and padded to give them a particular shape. *Reproduced by permission of © Historical Picture Archive/ CORBIS.*

separate leg hose into one garment, joined at the crotch. This allowed for full-length hose and shorter breeches, allowing more of the leg to be shown. Hose might be made in a variety of colors, though off-white seems to have been the most common.

Breeches, a form of pants, came in a wide variety of styles. The most common form of breech was called the trunk hose. Trunk hose were attached to the bottom of the doublet, a padded overshirt, with points, or small ties, and bagged outward before fastening on the upper leg. They looked almost like a puffy short skirt. Trunk hose were often worn with canions, a loose-fitting hose for the upper leg. An exaggerated form of trunk hose was known as pumpkin breeches. Made with contrasting vertical panels of fabric, these breeches ballooned outward, making it look as if the wearer had a large pumpkin about his waist. Venetians were a form of breeches that reached to the knee; they were padded at the waist and upper thigh and grew slimmer as they reached the knee. Pluderhose were baggy all the way from the waist to the knee, and the baggy fabric hung down to hide the fastening at the knee. The longest breeches, known as slops, reached all the way to the calf.

Breeches could be made from a variety of fabrics, including wool, cotton, silk, and velvet, and could be among the most intricate of men's garments. In many cases breeches were made in panels of alternating fabric, and they might be trimmed out with lace strips of fur. Very often breeches were padded with bombast, a form of stuffing, to give them a particular shape. Although padded breeches were most common among upper-class men, simple hose and breeches were worn by men of all classes.

FOR MORE INFORMATION

Bigelow, Marybelle S. *Fashion in History: Apparel in the Western World.* Minneapolis, MN: Burgess Publishing, 1970.

Cassin-Scott, Jack. *Costume and Fashion in Colour, 1550–1760.* Introduction by Ruth M. Green. Dorset, England: Blandford Press, 1975.

Payne, Blanche, Geitel Winakor, and Jane Farrell-Beck. *The History of Costume.* 2nd ed. New York: HarperCollins, 1992.

[*See also* **Volume 2, Europe in the Middle Ages: Hose and Breeches; Volume 3, Sixteenth Century: Bombast**]

Mandilion

Over the top of their doublets (a slightly padded overshirt) and jerkins (a close-fitting, often sleeveless, jacket), men of the sixteenth century wore a number of jackets or cloaks. These cloaks were worn for warmth but also for decoration. Some were made in a material that matched the wearer's hose. Late in the century one such cloak, called a mandilion, was used almost entirely for decorative purposes. The mandilion was a long-sleeved, hip-length cloak that opened down the front; it could be made of silk, velvet, linen, or other fabrics.

What made the mandilion unusual was the way it was worn, especially by the soldiers among whom it was popular. Instead of wearing it over both shoulders like a regular cloak, stylish men draped the mandilion over one shoulder, leaving one sleeve hanging down the front and the other down the back. For reasons that are not known, to wear the mandilion in this manner was called "Collie-Westonward." It became so common to wear the mandilion this way, according to fashion historian Virginia LaMar in *English Dress in the Age of Shakespeare,* that tailors eventually made the jackets with false sleeves since they were never used.

FOR MORE INFORMATION

LaMar, Virginia A. *English Dress in the Age of Shakespeare.* Washington, DC: Folger Shakespeare Library, 1958.

Payne, Blanche, Geitel Winakor, and Jane Farrell-Beck. *The History of Costume.* 2nd ed. New York: HarperCollins, 1992.

Ruffs

One of the most distinctive fashions of the late fifteenth and sixteenth centuries, the ruff was a wide pleated collar, often stiffened with starch or wire, which stood out like a wheel around the neck. Expensive and time-consuming to care for, the ruff was only for the wealthy. Ruffs had the effect of holding the head up in a proud and lordly pose, which made them popular with nobility across Europe. Both men and women wore the awkward ruff.

In the late 1400s the necklines on men's doublets, slightly padded short overshirts, and women's gowns opened to reveal the shirts worn underneath. These shirts were often closed at the neck by means of a drawstring laced through the edge of the fabric. When such a string was drawn tight, it produced a gathered ruffle around the neck. This ruffle soon became fashionable, and it grew in size until it became a separate piece of cloth or lace that was tied around the neck. The first wide ruffs appeared in Spain, but they soon spread to England, France, Italy, and Holland, where they remained popular well into the seventeenth century.

Over the course of their two-century history, ruffs varied greatly in size and style. They might be as narrow as an inch or as wide as twelve inches. Ruffs could be closed, which meant that they kept their flared shape all the way around the neck, or open, which meant that they extended to the sides and back only. Open ruffs allowed for easier movement of the head, and they allowed women to reveal their upper chests, or cleavage, as was fashionable in the late sixteenth and early seventeenth centuries. Especially after the introduction of starch in 1560, ruffs could be made to stand very stiffly away from the neck, though many people preferred a ruff that lay flat. Ruffs were often made of lace and paired with lace cuffs at the sleeves.

Ruffs created controversy in the sixteenth century. Protestant groups that protested against excesses in fashion singled out the ruff for criticism, calling the larger ruffs "millstones" or "cartwheels." Ruffs were somewhat impractical: they restricted movement considerably, and those who wore wide ruffs often had to eat with special long utensils so that they could reach their mouths. Some European governments tried to pass laws to restrict their size. Queen Elizabeth I of England, who ruled from 1558 to 1603 and who

The ruff was a wide pleated collar, often stiffened with starch or wire, which stood out like a wheel around the neck. Ruffs had the effect of holding the head up in a proud and lordly pose, which made them popular with nobility across Europe. *Courtesy of the Library of Congress.*

MEDICI COLLAR

The ultimate extension of the ruffs, or wide pleated collars, that were so popular among the wealthy in the sixteenth century was the Medici collar. A Medici collar provided a large, decorative frame around the sides and back of a woman's head. The collar was typically worn with a gown with a décolleté neckline, a low neckline that revealed a woman's cleavage. Supported by wire or heavy starch, these collars of lace, embroidered satin, or some other light material could reach great heights, towering over the shoulders and head of the wearer. They might be studded with tiny jewels and could be worn with a normal ruff if desired.

The Medici collar was introduced and named after Catherine de Médicis, who was Queen of France from 1560 to 1574. The collar may be most associated, however, with Elizabeth I of England (1533–1603), whose great flair for dramatic clothing styles made her the fashion trendsetter of the century. Medici collars have remained in use up to the present day, though they are now worn only in pageants or shows.

loved to wear ruffs herself, passed a law in 1580 that limited the size of ruffs worn by people outside her court. She even posted guards at the gates of the city of London in England to monitor the size of ruffs. Like most laws limiting clothing, called sumptuary laws, this law did not have much effect.

It took a lot of work to care for a ruff properly. They were preserved by servants in special boxes. Starch was painted on the white linen fabric used to make ruffs. The fabric was then carefully folded into pleats, sometimes in the shape of figure eights. They were then pressed and dried with a hot round rod called a goffering iron. The very wide cartwheel ruffs were too heavy for starch alone and required a metal framework over which the linen fabric was stretched.

FOR MORE INFORMATION

All the Rage. Alexandria, VA: Time-Life Books, 1992.

Cassin-Scott, Jack. *Costume and Fashion in Colour, 1550–1760.* Introduction by Ruth M. Green. Dorset, England: Blandford Press, 1975.

LaMar, Virginia A. *English Dress in the Age of Shakespeare.* Washington, DC: Folger Shakespeare Library, 1958.

Payne, Blanche, Geitel Winakor, and Jane Farrell-Beck. *The History of Costume.* 2nd ed. New York: HarperCollins, 1992.

Yarwood, Doreen. *The Encyclopedia of World Costume.* New York: Charles Scribner's Sons, 1978.

Sleeves

Fabric arm coverings, or sleeves, were an essential part of the clothing ensemble worn by both men and women during the Renaissance. Although sleeves were sometimes attached directly to men's doublets (overshirts) and jerkins (jackets) or to the bodice of women's gowns, just as often they were made separately and were attached to garments by means of points, or small ties at the connecting end of both garments. Because these sleeves were interchangeable, they could be worn with a variety of garments to create a different look.

Sleeves were an essential part of sixteenth-century fashion. Sometimes sleeves were attached directly to the clothing, and other times they were made separately and were attached by means of small ties. *Reproduced by permission of © Francis G. Mayer/CORBIS.*

There was a huge variety of sleeve styles that were worn during the sixteenth century and beyond. They all used some of the several distinctive sleeve styles, including puffs, panes, and padding. Puffs were large bunches of fabric that puffed out in a circle around the arm. They were most common at the top of the sleeve, near the shoulder, but could also appear at the elbow or at the wrist. One German sleeve of the midcentury featured a series of puffs all the way down the arm. Another common sleeve feature was panes. These were panels of fabric that ran the length of the sleeve. They might be in contrasting colors or fabrics and were sometimes pleated. A popular style of the late century was called rising panes and featured a series of panes caught into vertical puffs. Also late in the century padding and stiffening was added to allow sleeves to hold a rounded melon shape. All of these features were used to add volume to various parts of the arm.

Most sleeves combined puffs and panels with a length of sleeve that was very close fitting. These features were adorned with ribbons, jewels, slashing, a decorative technique that involved making small cuts in the outer fabric of a garment, and other decoration. Both men and women might also wear false sleeves along with regular sleeves. These attached at the shoulder but hung down behind the arm, often in large billows of fabric.

Sleeves were an essential part of the wardrobe, so they were made in the same rich fabrics as other garments, including silk and velvet. They often had fancy lace or linen cuffs attached to the ends of the sleeves.

FOR MORE INFORMATION

Cassin-Scott, Jack. *Costume and Fashion in Colour, 1550–1760.* Introduction by Ruth M. Green. Dorset, England: Blandford Press, 1975.

Payne, Blanche, Geitel Winakor, and Jane Farrell-Beck. *The History of Costume.* 2nd ed. New York: HarperCollins, 1992.

[*See also* **Volume 3, Fifteenth Century: Doublet; Volume 3, Seventeenth Century: Gowns**]

Sixteenth-Century Headwear

As in the preceding several centuries, the hairstyles worn during the sixteenth century were driven by the tastes of kings, queens, and their courts. During the early part of the century, for example, French king Francis I (1494–1547) wore his hair in a long bob and many in France followed his example. In 1521 an accident led to a portion of Francis's hair catching fire, and the king was forced to cut his hair short. Again, his court and many other Frenchmen followed suit. Henry VIII (1491–1547), the king of England, liked the new French style and cut his hair short. In fact, he liked his short hair so much that in 1535 he commanded everyone in his court to cut their hair as short as his. The trend toward short hair for men, usually worn no longer than the bottom of the ears, continued for the better part of the century. It was only very late in the century that men began to grow their hair long, and they would keep it long for nearly two centuries.

The same kings who liked short hair also preferred beards, and there were a great variety of beard styles worn throughout the century. Only older men and poor men wore long, poorly trimmed beards. Upper-class men and those who wanted to be fashionable trimmed their beards and mustaches neatly. Some of the most popular styles were the *pique devant,* a narrow beard that came to a point, and the spade, which was shaped like a slightly rounded shovel. Some men cut their beard off square and others were even known to wear a forked beard.

Men also wore a variety of hats. Early in the century simple bonnets or caps, low, soft hats with narrow brims, were most popular. After about the 1570s, however, larger hats became more popular. Hats could be made of felt, leather, or even fur. The copotain, a tall, round-crowned hat with a medium brim, was one of the most popular hats. Hats could be worn very simply, or they might be

Bobbed hair and beards, as seen here on Sir Francis Bacon, were very popular on men in the sixteenth century. *Courtesy of the Library of Congress.*

adorned with feathers, jewels, or decorative headbands.

Women continued to wear the large hats and headdresses of the previous century, but only in the earliest part of the sixteenth century. The custom that kept mature or married women from showing any of their hair in public was fading, and hat styles began to allow more of the hair to show. By midcentury hats and veiled headdresses, called lappets, and French hoods stood away from the forehead and temples to reveal rows of artfully curved hair. Very late in the century, and especially among royal women such as Queen Elizabeth (1533–1603) of England, small coronets (crowns) or jeweled hairpieces replaced the hat and allowed a nearly complete display of the hair. Elizabeth had dramatic red hair, but she was known to possess eighty wigs of varying color and style.

Women continued to wear their hair as they had during the fifteenth century: long and straight and styled with a variety of braids, curls, rolls, and other forms of wrapping. Metal hairpins were first used to keep hair in place in 1545, and by the end of the century women were using wire hair frames called palisades to give structure to their elaborately braided and styled hair. It was very common for women to add strings of jewels or flowers to their hair, or to string ribbons through their braids. Wigs or sections of false hair were also used when the woman's own hair was too thin or not long enough for the desired style. Also, many women used dyes or other methods to color their hair, with blond and red being favorite colors.

FOR MORE INFORMATION

Corson, Richard. *Fashions in Hair: The First Five Thousand Years.* London, England: Peter Owen, 2001.

Payne, Blanche, Geitel Winakor, and Jane Farrell-Beck. *The History of Costume.* 2nd ed. New York: HarperCollins, 1992.

Trasko, Mary. *Daring Do's: A History of Extraordinary Hair.* New York: Flammarion, 1994.

Copotain

One of the more common hats worn by men during the sixteenth century and into the seventeenth century was the copotain. Generally black in color and made of a thick felt, the copotain had a medium size brim, ranging between one and three inches, and a tall rounded crown. It was sometimes worn with a hatband, a band made of leather or fabric that ran around the crown just above the brim. Popular throughout Europe from about the 1550s onward, the hat became particularly associated with conservative gentlemen and was later adopted by Puritans, a very conservative, or traditional and opposed to change, Protestant religious group. Puritans wearing the

Popular throughout Europe from about the 1550s onward, the copotain hat first was associated with conservative gentlemen and later was adopted by Puritans. *Reproduced by permission of © Bettmann/CORBIS.*

hat in the British colonies in North America in the seventeenth century often had a simple buckle on the front of their hatband.

FOR MORE INFORMATION

Cassin-Scott, Jack. *Costume and Fashion in Colour, 1550–1760.* Introduction by Ruth M. Green. Dorset, England: Blandford Press, 1975.

Payne, Blanche, Geitel Winakor, and Jane Farrell-Beck. *The History of Costume.* 2nd ed. New York: HarperCollins, 1992.

Hair Coloring

From as early as the founding of the Roman Empire in 27 B.C.E. women have been known to color their hair. Blonde has often been the most sought after color, perhaps because it resembles gold, perhaps because it is the least common natural color. Europeans in the sixteenth century were no different, though they did pursue new ways to lighten their hair. Women living in the Italian city of Venice in the late sixteenth century were known to sit all day in the blazing sun wearing a special crownless hat that allowed the hair to stick out the top and be bleached by the sun, yet kept the rest of the face covered. One contemporary observer, quoted in Richard Corson's *Fashions in Hair,* tells of a Venetian woman who sat in the hot sun so long that, "although she obtained the effect of her desires [blond hair], yet withall, shee procured to her selfe a violent Head ach, and bled almost every day abundantly through the Nose; and on a time being desirous to stop the Blood by pressing of her Nostrils, not farr from her right Eye toward her Temple, . . . as it were by a hole made with a needles point, the Blood burst out abundantly." Women in northern Europe, where the sun was not so constant, sought out various dyes for their hair, which had become sophisticated enough to allow women to obtain a variety of different shades of blond.

FOR MORE INFORMATION

Corson, Richard. *Fashions in Hair: The First Five Thousand Years.* London, England: Peter Owen, 2001.

Trasko, Mary. *Daring Do's: A History of Extraordinary Hair.* New York: Flammarion, 1994.

Palisades

One of the major trends of the late sixteenth century was for women to expose more of their hair and to wear more elaborate hairstyles. Borrowing from the tradition of creating massive shaped hats with the use of wire cages, such as the steeple and ram's horn headdresses of the fourteenth and fifteenth centuries, women began to use stiff wire to give structure to their hair. These wire structures were called palisades after the word for a fence of stakes used for defensive purposes in war. The term palisades was probably not coined by women who liked the fancy hairstyles, but rather by those who thought the styles were excessive and silly.

Women and their servants could use palisades in a number of ways. A common use of wire was to create a kind of dome above the forehead and to attach a linen cloth that flowed over the back of the head, revealing the hair beneath. Women might also braid their hair around a wire framework. The wires allowed the hair to take a variety of shapes that would be impossible without the underlying structure. Wire was also used with pads to give extra volume to the hairstyles and as an anchor for the strings of jewels and ribbons used to create the elaborate hairstyles of the late sixteenth and seventeenth centuries.

FOR MORE INFORMATION

Corson, Richard. *Fashions in Hair: The First Five Thousand Years.* London, England: Peter Owen, 2001.

Payne, Blanche, Geitel Winakor, and Jane Farrell-Beck. *The History of Costume.* 2nd ed. New York: HarperCollins, 1992.

Trasko, Mary. *Daring Do's: A History of Extraordinary Hair.* New York: Flammarion, 1994.

[*See also* **Volume 2, Europe in the Middle Ages: Ram's Horn Headdress; Volume 2, Europe in the Middle Ages: Steeple Headdress**]

Sixteenth-Century Body Decorations

The personal grooming habits of people in the sixteenth century seem strange to us today. On the one hand, wealthy people took great care with their hairstyles and, in the case of women, with their makeup. On the other hand, the practice of bathing was infrequent among even the wealthiest people and quite rare among the poorer classes. Europeans in the sixteenth century simply misunderstood the nature of disease and believed that they could get sick if they used water to clean themselves. Other than this odd belief, Europeans from this period took great care with their appearance and with the accessories that they chose.

The use of makeup was widespread among wealthier women in the kingdoms of Europe. The most common form of makeup was white pancake makeup applied to the face, with bright red rouge used to color the lips and the cheeks. As fashion historian Ruth M. Green noted in the introduction to *Costume and Fashion in Colour, 1550–1760,* by Jack Cassin-Scott, the contrast of these colors would have made women look doll-like in bright light, but probably appeared more subtle in the candlelit castles of the time. The cosmetics used during this period were based on poisonous preparations of lead and quite unhealthy.

Both men and women wore a number of accessories as part of their typical outfit. For men, the most common accessories were a belt, a sword, and a pair of gloves. Men wore a simple leather belt from which they hung their sword, an item that no gentleman would do without. The sword might be highly ornamented, with its sheath and handle bearing jewels or other decoration. Men also tucked their leather gloves into their belt. Women carried a range of accessories, including fans, soft Cordoba leather gloves, and handkerchiefs. One of the most unique fashion accessories was the pomander, a metal or gold ball that contained perfume and was attached to the belt

HYGIENE

The definition of hygiene, or personal cleanliness, has varied from culture to culture throughout history. However, one thing is clear: contrary to popular belief, people have not become cleaner over time. Many factors, including local customs, the outbreak of disease, scientific knowledge, and religious beliefs, have affected the ways people clean their bodies and clothes and dispose of their wastes.

The idea of regular bathing as an important part of personal hygiene is not a modern one. Ancient Romans bathed themselves regularly in large public baths before the first century C.E. In Europe during the Middle Ages (c. 500–c. 1500) there were also many public bathhouses, called "stews" by the common people who used them. In the early 1300s some European monks, men who dedicated their lives to the Catholic Church by joining religious orders, had plumbing that brought water for bathing inside the monasteries where they

lived. However, the bubonic plague, a very contagious, often fatal bacterial disease which swept much of the world during the fourteenth century and was also known as the Black Death, caused the closure of many public gathering places, including the public baths. People believed that public baths may have caused the disease, inspiring in many Europeans a fear of using water to clean the body. Some Christians had long believed that submerging the body in water could wash away the holy water of the baptism ritual. After the arrival of the plague, this mistrust of water increased. Many people believed that placing water on the skin would open the pores, allowing disease to enter the body. Alongside these superstitions there was good reason to doubt the safety of water. During the 1400s and 1500s plumbing was fairly primitive and, in large cities, sewage flowed down streets and gutters in open streams that smelled bad and carried disease. Even the water from wells could be contaminated, and no way to purify such water had yet been discovered.

with a cord or tie. Many women of the time are pictured holding the pomander near their nose, perhaps to ward off the smells of body odor that must have filled the air. Because of this lack of sanitation, men and women alike also draped flea furs about their necks to attract the fleas that infested their clothes away from other parts of their body.

"As for jewellery (sic)," writes Ruth M. Green, "there could hardly be too much of it" for both men and women. Men wore rings, long dangling neck chains, pendants, and even jeweled earrings. Women also wore rings on every finger and even the thumb, as well as bracelets and necklaces. Goldworking skills were highly refined during the era, and widespread exploration and trade made a variety of jewels available to the wealthiest people. Perhaps the most striking use of jewels during this period was as ornamentation for garments. Nearly every garment worn could be enhanced by jewels sewn onto the surface or worn on belts or garters around the

Rather than washing in water, the preferred way of cleansing the body during the sixteenth century was to wipe it with white linen cloths, which were thought to have healing properties. The poor had little linen and no servants to keep it clean and white. They also had little leisure time for bathing or washing clothes. It became common among the poor to bathe only twice a year, once in the spring and once in the fall, though the face, hands, and teeth were usually cleaned daily. The teeth were usually brushed with a chewed twig, then wiped with cloth. The wealthy bathed more frequently, sometimes weekly or monthly. In addition, their servants kept them supplied with clean white linen, both to wipe their bodies and to wear. While most nobles wore clean linen every day, other clothes were seldom washed. The very wealthy simply gave away their clothes when they were too dirty to wear.

Soap had been invented in the Orient and brought back to Europe during the eleventh century by soldiers returning from the religious Crusades to extract control of the Holy Land from the Muslims who lived there. The new soaps were expensive, however, and even the king seldom used them. Instead, most of the royalty and nobility concealed the smell of imperfectly cleaned bodies with a variety of strong perfumes. Most wealthy people carried bottles of perfume, pomanders (scented jeweled balls), or scented handkerchiefs with them at all times. The poor simply smelled.

The idea that germs cause disease and infection, and that cleanliness can prevent the spread of germs, was not widely understood until the 1800s, but a sixteenth-century French doctor named Ambroise Paré (1510–1590) did discover the value of cleanliness in treating wounds. On the battlefield Paré ran out of boiling oil, the usual treatment for soldiers' wounds, and treated his remaining patients by simply washing their wounds with water. When he discovered that the washed wounds healed, while those treated with oil got worse, he spread the word. Doctors throughout Europe soon stopped using the boiling oil treatment in favor of water.

sleeves, legs, or waist. Women often laced strings of pearls into their hair, and ruffs, wide pleated collars, and high collars were also studded with small pearls and jewels.

The jewelry, accessories, and makeup discussed were used only by the wealthy people who attended the courts of the kings and queens of Europe and perhaps by the wealthiest merchants of European cities. Most ordinary people in the sixteenth century could not afford and would have had little use for these impractical elements of costume.

FOR MORE INFORMATION

Cassin-Scott, Jack. *Costume and Fashion in Colour, 1550–1760.* Introduction by Ruth M. Green. Dorset, England: Blandford Press, 1975.

Chamberlin, E. R. *Everyday Life in Renaissance Times.* London, England: B. T. Batsford, 1967.

Cosgrave, Bronwyn. *The Complete History of Costume and Fashion: From Ancient Egypt to the Present Day.* New York: Checkmark Books, 2000.

Payne, Blanche, Geitel Winakor, and Jane Farrell-Beck. *The History of Costume.* 2nd ed. New York: HarperCollins, 1992.

Taylor, Laurence. *Everyday Life: The Sixteenth Century.* Morristown, NJ: Silver Burdett, 1983.

Cordoba Leather Gloves

Among the many accessories that both men and women might carry in the sixteenth century were finely made Cordoba leather gloves. People carried a variety of gloves during the time period, including gloves made from leather, suede (leather with a rough surface), or kid (the skin of a young goat), but the most prized gloves were made of leather from Cordoba, Spain. Cordoba had been a center for leather tanning since the eighth century C.E., and it was known for the outstanding quality of its leathers, which came in a variety of colors. A fancy pair of gloves had delicately sewn fingers and might be perfumed. Some gloves had long gauntlets, or decorative extensions that extended beyond the wrist. These gauntlets might have fringes or scallops and could be embroidered or studded with jewels.

The fanciest Cordoba leather gloves were probably never worn. Instead they were carried as a pair, either held gracefully in the hand or tucked into a decorative belt worn around the waist. The gloves that people actually wore for work, riding, or bird handling were made of more common leather.

FOR MORE INFORMATION

Payne, Blanche, Geitel Winakor, and Jane Farrell-Beck. *The History of Costume.* 2nd ed. New York: HarperCollins, 1992.

Yarwood, Doreen. *The Encyclopedia of World Costume.* New York: Charles Scribner's Sons, 1978.

Fans

Fashionable ladies in the sixteenth and seventeenth centuries were known for carrying a variety of personal accessories, including gloves, pomanders (scented jeweled balls), handkerchiefs, and fans. Fans had been used in China from as early as 3000 B.C.E. and were popular in Japan beginning in the seventh century C.E. People began to use feather fans during the Middle Ages (c. 500–c. 1500) and the rigid board fan, usually made of decorated wood, came into use in Italy early in the sixteenth century. The folding fan was imported to Europe from the Orient in the sixteenth century and quickly became popular among noblewomen in the courts of Spain, Portugal, Italy, France, and England.

As with other elements of costume from this period, decoration was the key to the fan. Fans could be made of all variety of materials, from exotic bird feathers to delicate lace to gilded wood. No expense was spared to make fans for the richest women. The way that a fan was used was also an important part of a woman's overall presentation. A woman might shyly hide her face behind a spread fan, or wave her fan about in a dramatic manner.

FOR MORE INFORMATION

De Vere Green, Bertha. *Fans Over the Ages: A Collector's Guide.* New York: A. S. Barnes, 1979.

Yarwood, Doreen. *The Encyclopedia of World Costume.* New York: Charles Scribner's Sons, 1978.

[*See also* **Volume 2, Early Asian Cultures: Fans**]

Flea Fur

More than any other garment, the flea fur helps us to understand just how different living conditions were in sixteenth-century Europe. People of the period did not bathe very often, and they rarely washed their clothes or bedsheets. The conditions were

perfect for infestations of fleas, small bloodsucking insects that live on the bodies of warm-blooded animals like humans. Even the wealthiest people had to endure frequent bites from fleas. One of the ways that they combated the pests was with flea fur.

A flea fur was made from the pelt of a small furry animal like a mink, an ermine, or a ferret. It was worn about the neck in the hopes that the fleas would prefer the thick and smelly fur of the animal to the smooth and smelly skin of a human. Wealthy people added ornaments to their flea furs, including jeweled clasps and golden chains. It is unknown whether poor people wore shabbier flea furs made from the pelts of rats and other less desirable rodents or simply endured the flea bites.

One of the ways that sixteenth-century Europeans combated fleas was with flea fur, which was worn about the neck in the hopes that the fleas would prefer the thick fur of the animal to the skin of a human. *Reproduced by permission of © Archivo Iconografico, S.A./CORBIS.*

FOR MORE INFORMATION

Wilcox, R. Turner. *The Mode in Furs: The History of Furred Costume of the World from the Earliest Times to the Present.* New York: Scribner, 1951.

Yarwood, Doreen. *The Encyclopedia of World Costume.* New York: Charles Scribner's Sons, 1978.

Handkerchiefs

One of the true fashion innovations of the sixteenth century was the introduction of the handkerchief as a fashion accessory. Handkerchiefs themselves were not new; people had been carrying a small cloth for blowing their nose for years. These soiled items, however, were kept tucked away out of sight, causing uncertainty as to when the first handkerchief was actually invented. In the sixteenth century, however, the handkerchief came out of the pocket and into public scrutiny. The same women who dressed in exquisite silk gowns with delicate lace ruffs, or collars, and cuffs had their tailors add lace or a scalloped edge to a fine linen cloth and elevated the handkerchief to the status of fashion accessory. A fine lacy handkerchief, or hanky, was not tucked away in a pocket but held in the hand or draped coyly across the arm. It might be matched with a fan or another accessory.

Handkerchiefs have remained a fashion accessory ever since. It is rumored in fashion history that Frenchwoman Marie Antoinette (1755–1793) was frustrated that handkerchiefs were offered in so many shapes: round, oval, rectangular, and so on. Her husband, King Louis XVI of France (1754–1793), made it a law that all handkerchiefs must be square, and they have remained square ever since. During the twentieth century it became fashionable for men to place a handkerchief in the left breast pocket of their suit coat with just an inch of the fabric sticking out of the pocket. Carefully folded and ironed, these breast-pocket handkerchiefs could come in a variety of colors, though white was preferred. Though people no longer dangle a handkerchief from their hand as a fashion gesture, the handkerchief has remained a common item for personal use to this day, though facial tissue is now more commonly used.

In the sixteenth century, the handkerchief was made from fine cloth and decorated with lace or a scalloped edge, elevating it to the status of fashion accessory. *Reproduced by permission of © Gianni Dagli Orti/CORBIS.*

FOR MORE INFORMATION

Bigelow, Marybelle S. *Fashion in History: Apparel in the Western World.* Minneapolis, MN: Burgess Publishing, 1970.

Cassin-Scott, Jack. *Costume and Fashion in Colour, 1550–1760.* Introduction by Ruth M. Green. Dorset, England: Blandford Press, 1975.

Gustafson, Helen. *Hanky Panky: An Intimate History of the Handkerchief.* Berkeley, CA: Ten Speed Press, 2002.

Sixteenth-Century Footwear

By the sixteenth century footwear construction methods had grown quite advanced. The shoes of common people were generally made of leather, and while they were fairly simple in construction they were also very durable. Soles were made of wood, cork, or extra layers of leather, and uppers, or the tops of shoes, were either tied or buckled in place. Shoemakers, called cobblers, also developed the ability to make very tall boots for riding or fieldwork. These boots came up to the thigh and had a floppy leather cuff that could be rolled down. In the next century these boots would become fancier in their design and were commonly worn by men of the upper class. In the sixteenth century, however, they were still used primarily for outdoor work or by members of mounted military units.

The footwear of the upper classes was usually far from practical. In keeping with the century's trend toward rich fabrics and elaborate ornament, both men and women wore shoes that emphasized fashion over comfort or ease of use. Men in the early

Most wealthy men of the sixteenth century wore slippers made of soft leather, silk, or velvet, often in patterns matched to their outfits. *Reproduced by permission of © Gianni Dagli Orti/CORBIS.*

part of the century were fond of very wide-toed shoes. Leather slip-ons, called duck's bill shoes, flared out at the toe. In their most extreme form they could be as wide as twelve inches at the toe and forced men to walk like a duck. This fashion faded by midcentury, and most wealthy men wore slippers made of soft leather, silk, or velvet, often in patterns matched to their outfit. Women also adopted an extremely impractical form of shoe called the chopine. These slippers sat atop a platform that ran the length of the shoe and could be as high as twenty-four inches. Chopines were very difficult to walk in. People of both sexes also began to wear shoes with thicker heels, including the first wedge heels. Both men and women used ribbons, bows, and jewels to decorate their shoes. Such shoes were not intended for outdoor wear, of course, and both sexes wore overshoes called pattens and pantofles to protect their dainty shoes if they did go outside in them.

FOR MORE INFORMATION

Cassin-Scott, Jack. *Costume and Fashion in Colour, 1550–1760.* Introduction by Ruth M. Green. Dorset, England: Blandford Press, 1975.

Lawlor, Laurie. *Where Will This Shoe Take You?: A Walk Through the History of Footwear.* New York: Walker and Co., 1996.

Chopines

Chopines (sha-PEENS), shoes with very tall wooden or cork platform soles, inspired what some consider the first clothing fad. During the High Renaissance of the sixteenth century, fashionable, wealthy women in Venice, Italy, eagerly climbed into these shoes that ranged from six to twenty-four inches in height. Feet were secured to the pedestals with straps of leather or uppers (the part of a shoe above the sole) made of silk or other fabric. The tops of chopines were rarely seen; the shoes were more valued for their height and for the dainty stride they required of wearers. Towering on their shoes in glamorous long gowns, women who wore chopines needed the support of their husbands or maids to hobble the streets and royal courts of Venice.

Chopines made Italian women "half flesh, half wood," remarked traveler John Evelyn in his diary of 1666, as quoted in *The Book of Costume.*

The craze for chopines in Italy coincided with the peak of attraction for extravagant dress during the 1500s, when almost every article of clothing was highly exaggerated. By the late sixteenth and early seventeenth century, Spanish, French, and Swiss women were also teetering fashionably on chopines. The fad never reached northern Europe.

Chopines were not an Italian invention. The shoes signaled the establishment of trade between Venetian merchants and the Near East, or southwest Asia. Although the true origins of chopines is not known, the tall clogs Turkish women wore in bathhouses or the pedestal shoes worn by actors on Greek stages in early history may have been the inspiration for chopines. Chopines were used by the Manchus (people native to Manchuria who ruled China from 1644 to 1912) in China in the mid-1600s as a less painful alternative to the deforming effects of foot binding that had been practiced since the tenth century. (Foot binding was a common practice in China whereby young women and girls would bind their feet so as to make them stop growing.) The pedestals of Chinese chopines were much slimmer than those developed in Venice, offering women a footprint similar to that of bound feet and giving them the same difficulty walking.

Although enjoyed for their glamorous, fashionable effect, chopines were considered by some observers as tools to keep women in the home, to keep them from wandering, going astray morally. Indeed, this was the purpose of the foot binding that chopines replaced in China, and chopines did make walking a slow and difficult task. In Italy clergymen regarded the wearing of chopines as particularly admirable because the shoes inhibited the wearer from indulging in morally dangerous pleasures such as dance.

FOR MORE INFORMATION

Contini, Mila. *Fashion: From Ancient Egypt to the Present Day.* Edited by James Laver. New York: Odyssey Press, 1965.

Cosgrave, Bronwyn. *The Complete History of Costume and Fashion: From Ancient Egypt to the Present Day.* New York: Checkmark Books, 2000.

Kybalová, Ludmila, Olga Herbenová, and Milena Lamarová. *The Pictorial Encyclopedia of Fashion.* Translated by Claudia Rosoux. London, England: Paul Hamlyn, 1968.

Wilton, Mary Margaret Stanley Egerton, Countess of, and R. L. Shep. *The Book of Costume: Or Annals of Fashion (1846) by a Lady of Rank.* Lopez Island, WA: R. L. Shep, 1986.

Pattens and Pantofles

The sixteenth century was not known for its practical footwear. The shoes that most wealthy people wore indoors were either very delicate, perhaps made of silk or velvet, or very cumbersome, like the extremely high chopines worn by women. When people wanted to walk outdoors they turned to practical footwear like pattens and pantofles. Pattens were a heavy-duty outer shoe, usually made out of wood, that strapped on over the top of regular shoes. Some pattens might have a wooden sole to which was attached a metal ring several inches tall that elevated the wearer above the mud and dust of the street. Pantofles were much more delicate, resembling the garden clogs or scuffs (flat-soled slipper) of the modern day. They usually slipped on the foot and had a cork sole. By the end of the century pantofles were made of materials nearly as delicate as indoor shoes and could be highly ornate. Still, they offered protection for the feet, their main purpose.

FOR MORE INFORMATION

Cassin-Scott, Jack. *Costume and Fashion in Colour, 1550–1760.* Introduction by Ruth M. Green. Dorset, England: Blandford Press, 1975.

LaMar, Virginia A. *English Dress in the Age of Shakespeare.* Washington, DC: Folger Shakespeare Library, 1958.

[*See also* **Volume 3, Sixteenth Century: Chopines**]

The Seventeenth Century

European history in the seventeenth century was dominated on the one hand by the rise of France as the greatest power in the region, and on the other hand by the great fight for political power that occurred between the monarch and the governing body of Parliament in England. These were the great social issues of the age, and they had a great influence on the way people lived and dressed. More subtle historical changes, such as the growth of the middle class and the growing differences between a luxurious Catholic and a plain Protestant sense of style also had an enduring influence on European culture and costume.

The rise of the French

The century began with power in Europe fairly evenly distributed between France, England, and Spain, but that balance would soon end. The Thirty Years' War (1618–48) was fought in Germany between the Spanish, French, Swedish, and Danish. By the end of the conflict Spain's influence beyond its borders had diminished significantly. France, on the other hand, became a great power, expanding its territory on all sides. The war also led to the creation of the Dutch Republic, or Netherlands, which became a powerful economic force during the century and beyond.

With England distracted by years of civil war and political strife, France became the reigning power of Europe. French king Louis XIV (1638–1715), who ruled from 1643 to 1715, slowly won power from the nobles and established himself as the most powerful monarch in the region. He formed a huge army, crushed internal resistance, and fought to expand his territories. He also built France into an economic power by refusing to import goods from other countries and by encouraging French industries to become Europe's biggest producers of luxury goods. Soon, France became the leading producer of such luxury items as lace, silk, ribbons, and wigs, exporting them to the rest of Europe. French political and economic power was thus used to influence taste, for all of Europe followed the fashions introduced in the French court and sold by French industries.

Years of strife in England

While France strengthened its power, England immersed itself in internal strife. The great conflict of the century was over whether the king or Parliament, which represented not the broad populace but a fairly select group of nobles and landowners, would have the greater power. This conflict was made worse by religious differences, with Catholic-sympathizing or openly Catholic kings pitted against a population that was increasingly Protestant. Long simmering political battles erupted into civil war in 1642, a conflict that ended in 1648 and was capped in January of 1649 by the beheading of Charles I, who reigned from 1625 until his death. After nearly two decades more of conflicted rule under Commonwealth chairman Oliver Cromwell (ruled 1649–60), King Charles II (reigned 1660–85), and King James II (reigned 1685–88), matters were settled with the establishment of the Protestant joint rulers William III (reigned 1689–1702) and Mary II (reigned 1689–94). Political power in England was effectively transferred to Parliament after 1689, thus creating the first representative government in Europe. Political stability and the defeat of the French in the Nine Years War (1688–97) set the stage for England to become the great world power for the next two centuries.

Though the English conflict was primarily about political power, religion played an important role in the conflict and in Europe as a whole. In general, the continent was increasingly divided into a Protestant north (England, Scotland, Ireland, the Dutch

DECLINE OF SUMPTUARY LAWS

A shopkeeper in London in 1600 could not purchase a silk doublet without threat of being fined or even thrown in prison, for laws on record throughout Europe set restrictions on the kinds of clothes and accessories that could be worn by those outside the ranks of nobles, such as knights, dukes, and earls. In England, King Henry VII (reigned 1509–47) and later his daughter, Queen Elizabeth I (reigned 1558–1603), passed a series of laws that restricted the use of certain luxurious textiles such as silk, satin, velvet, and other fabrics to people above certain ranks, such as knight or earl. Elizabeth also passed laws regulating the length of swords and the size of ruffs worn around the neck. Similar laws existed across Europe and in the British colonies in the New World. One law in Massachusetts made it a crime for anyone who possessed an estate below the value of two hundred British pounds to wear clothes made of certain fabrics.

Laws that regulate the types and styles of clothing that could be worn by certain people, as well as other luxuries, are called sumptuary laws. They had existed in Europe hundreds of years, but they reached their peak in the 1500s and early 1600s. Judging from the explosion of sumptuary laws passed during these years, European rulers thought it was very important to keep common people from consuming the clothes and other luxury goods enjoyed by the wealthiest classes. The higher classes were threatened because merchants and skilled workers had more income than ever before and found that by purchasing certain clothes they could appear wealthier than they really were. Rulers and nobles wanted to keep social distinctions clear, and they used sumptuary laws to do so.

Sumptuary laws were also used to help encourage local industries. The French, for example, placed a ban on lace from other countries, and local lace industries prospered as a result. Similar laws were passed in Spain, England, and other countries to promote local production of certain garments or textiles (fabrics). Sometimes these laws were just a reflection of patriotism or hostility towards another country.

By the mid-sixteenth century most European rulers came to accept that sumptuary laws didn't work and never had. People simply ignored the laws, which were nearly impossible to enforce. James I, who ruled England from 1603 to 1625, repealed most of the laws in his country, fearing that they were out of tune with the need for freedom for his people. After this time sumptuary laws became much more rare, though they were still used by rulers intent on enforcing class divisions in their society. The primary obstacle to poor people wearing the clothes of the rich throughout more recent history, however, has been the cost of the clothing and fabrics.

Republic, the German states, Sweden, and Denmark) and a Catholic south (France, Spain, Portugal, and Italy). Within England, those who supported a strong monarch tended to be Catholics, while those who supported representative government tended to be Protestants. Accordingly, northern nations tended toward representative forms of government, while southern nations favored a strong monarch closely allied to the leadership of the Catholic Church. The very different religious and political ideas of Protestants and Catholics contributed to real cultural differences between north and south and were eventually reflected in clothing styles as well. Over time, Protestants, and especially the more extreme Puritans, tended toward simplicity and austerity in their clothing styles, while Catholics tended toward luxury and extravagance.

Economic expansion

Other large-scale changes also had an impact on costume. Perhaps the most important was the continuing expansion of the role of shopkeepers, small landowners, professionals, and skilled workers. The members of this growing middle class of people played an ever more important role in the cultural and economic life of European countries, especially in Protestant countries. The middle classes had greater access to wealth, and their efforts to build businesses and progress financially fueled the economies of every nation. The largest industry in all of Europe was the textile, or fabric, industry, and many people who once worked on farms found employment in this industry, usually by spinning and weaving cloth in their homes in what was known as the putting-out system. One of the biggest innovations of this industry was the creation of something called "new draperies," a new form of lightweight wool. This adaptable and inexpensive material was used to make clothing for middle-class people, allowing them to wear decent clothing. There remained, of course, large numbers of people in every country who were very poor and who could not afford even this new, cheaper clothing. They had to rely on coarse wool and secondhand clothes.

Exploration and colonization continued to play a large role in Europe's affairs in this century. The New World, Spain, Portugal, France, the Dutch Republic, and England all nurtured colonies and fought with each other for control of the larger region. These colonies began to develop cultures and economies of their own during this century, though they mostly reflected the interests and culture of their mother country.

FOR MORE INFORMATION

Cameron, Euan, ed. *Early Modern Europe: An Oxford History.* Oxford and New York: Oxford University Press, 1999.

Cook, Chris, and Philip Broadhead. *The Longman Handbook of Early Modern Europe, 1453–1763.* New York: Longman, 2001.

Gerdes, Louise I., ed. *The 1600s.* San Diego, CA: Greenhaven Press, 2001.

Hunt, Alan. *Governance of the Consuming Passions: A History of Sumptuary Law.* New York: St. Martin's Press, 1996.

Secara, Maggie. *Elizabethan Sumptuary Statutes.* http://renaissance.dm.net/sumptuary (accessed on August 6, 2003).

Williams, E.N., ed. *The Facts on File Dictionary of European History.* New York: Facts on File, 1980.

Seventeenth-Century Clothing

The clothing worn by Europeans during the seventeenth century was influenced by fashion trends—rapid changes in style influenced by trendsetters—as never before. During the course of the century garments went from restrictive to comfortable and back to restrictive again, and excessive ornament was both stripped away and added back to clothing for both men and women. While the very wealthy continued to determine the styles that were most popular, political preferences and the rise of the middle classes also began to have a significant influence on fashion.

From ornamentation to elegance

Fashions in the early seventeenth century continued the trends of the previous century: men's doublets and women's bodices were worn tight and stiffened with rigid stays or padding; women's skirts were given full, rigid shapes with the help of farthingales, or hoops; and the garments of both sexes were laden with ornamentation, from jewelry to lace to the showiness of multiple contrasting fabrics. By the 1620s, however, styles began to change fairly dramatically. While the garments worn remained the same, such as the doublet, breeches, and hose for men and long gowns for women, the overall trend through the midcentury was toward softness and comfort. To allow for easier movement, waistlines on doublets and women's bodices rose higher, and the padding on both doublets and bodices was removed. The starched ruffs and whisks that once encircled the neck were replaced with the softer, more comfortable falling and standing bands. Women's sleeves began to rise, showing first the wrist and then the entire forearm. With the exception of petticoat breeches, men's breeches lost their bagginess and became slimmer and easier to move in. People continued to value rich materials and

FIRST FASHION PUBLICATIONS

Finding out what the latest fashions were before the seventeenth century was fairly difficult. Members of royalty—kings, queens, princes, and princesses—set fashion trends, and one had to actually see noblemen or women to get an idea of new trends. Some royals sent their tailors around the country with life-size dolls dressed in the latest styles to spread news of fashion changes. Then, in 1672, the first fashion magazine began publication in France. Called *Mercure Galant,* the magazine began to regularly offer comment on the latest clothing styles and was read throughout Europe. The French also led the way in the creation and circulation of fashion plates, beautiful illustrations of the latest garments that guided the work of tailors. (The term "fashion plate" would later be used to describe someone who was always dressed in style.) By the end of the century, many Parisian printers began selling fashion plates, or engravings of fashionable clothes. The trend has not yet stopped, with fashion magazines, such as *Elle* and *Vogue,* selling internationally by the millions in the twenty-first century.

exquisite design, but they set aside the rigid formality of earlier years and didn't add ornament for ornament's sake. Overall, the trend through the first sixty years of the century was toward looseness, comfort, and elegance.

French influence

These changes in fashion reflected the rising influence of France, with its freer sense of style, and the shrinking influence of Spain, with its stiff formality. French King Louis XIV (1638–1715), who ruled from 1643 to 1715, helped make France the leading fashion influence of the century. Louis believed that he could best lead his country by setting an example of style and taste in everything from architecture and furniture to food and fashion. He surrounded himself with a huge court of officers and advisers and held numerous lavish balls at which wealthy nobles competed to wear the most tasteful and elegant clothes. Louis's palace at Versailles became the center for French fashion. At the same time, France became Europe's leading producer of luxury goods. French cities led the production of silk, lace, and brocade, and they aggressively exported these materials to other countries, expanding their influence. France also exported its fashion in other ways as well such as through fashion publications.

Cavalier versus Roundhead

Though the preferred styles were simpler than in the sixteenth century, French fashions were still quite ornate. In fact, the French love of sumptuous fabrics and carefully chosen accessories led to a revival of fashion excess after about 1660. Stomachers stiffened and lengthened once more, and the overall profile of both men's and women's garments emphasized vertical lines that made wearers look tall and slim. For women tall hairstyles, high-heeled shoes, and long skirt extensions, called trains, all added to the effect. Ornament, in the form of decorated swords and baldrics, fancy lace collars, and high rolled boots, came back into style.

While the new lavish clothing styles were adopted by some, others rejected the excessive ornamentation in favor of more restrained styles. Throughout the century people's clothing styles diverged along these artistic lines. But clothing styles during the seventeenth century were not merely about looks; a person's choice of clothing also told the world about his or her religious or political positions.

Those who favored the new lavish clothing styles came to be known as Cavaliers, after those well-dressed soldiers who fought in support of the Catholic King Charles I in the English Civil War (1642–48). The Cavalier style soon was associated with a political position that favored the Catholic religion and a strong king. But not all followed this style or this political position. Another group, named after the Roundheads, who fought in support of Parliament, or the governing body in England, in the English Civil War, favored Protestant religions and wanted to give more political power to the people, especially by strengthening representative bodies like the English Parliament. The Roundheads soon developed a style sense of their own. They avoided the ornamentation and excess associated with Cavaliers, instead preferring more sober colors and less decorated fabrics. The most notable fashion innovation associated with the Roundheads was the introduction of the waistcoat and justaucorps as common men's garments, replacing or worn over top of the doublet.

The most extreme Roundheads were the Puritans, a strict religious sect that held strong ideas about avoiding excess in personal display. Puritans favored black clothes, simple fasteners, and clean lines. Being a Roundhead or a Puritan did not mean that one did not care about fashion, however. Roundheads valued rich if not ornate materials, and the richer followers of this style hired skilled tailors to give their garments a fine cut and finish. The split in fashion sense between the Cavaliers, who were most numerous in the Catholic countries of France, Spain, and Italy, and among Catholic sympathizers in England, and the Roundheads, who lived in the more heavily Protestant countries of England, Scotland, Germany, and Flanders (present-day Holland and Belgium), was one of the major fashion facts of the century.

Quickly changing fashions

The powerful influence of French fashion and the conflicting attractions of the Cavalier and Roundhead styles contributed to a quickening of the pace of change in the world of fashion. Another factor was the rising power of the middle class. Throughout the European countries shopkeepers, lawyers, doctors, and other skilled workers gained access to greater wealth and were able to afford more

Although the clothing of the seventeenth century required rich, textured fabrics and elegant trim, the overall trend was toward softness and comfort. *Reproduced by permission of © Stapleton Collection/CORBIS.*

expensive clothes. They soon mimicked the styles of the nobles, and the nobles in turn developed new clothing customs to set themselves apart. Styles changed much more quickly. One fashion historian marked seven changes in sleeve style in a two-year span. It became harder and harder to keep up with the latest fashions. Rulers made laws, called sumptuary laws, in order to keep "common" people from wearing the clothes favored by the wealthy, but these laws were ineffective and difficult to enforce. The poorer people remained outside the fashion loop, and continued to wear simplified versions of the garments of the wealthy in everyday fabrics such as wool and cotton.

FOR MORE INFORMATION

Contini, Mila. *Fashion: From Ancient Egypt to the Present Day.* Edited by James Laver. New York: Odyssey Press, 1965.

Cosgrave, Bronwyn. *The Complete History of Costume and Fashion: From Ancient Egypt to the Present Day.* New York: Checkmark Books, 2000.

Cunnington, C. Willett, and Phillis Cunnington. *Handbook of English Costume in the Seventeenth Century.* Boston, MA: Plays, Inc., 1972.

Hart, Avril, and Susan North. *Fashion in Detail: From the 17th and 18th Centuries.* New York: Rizzoli, 1998.

Hatt, Christine. *Clothes of the Early Modern World.* Columbus, OH: Peter Bedrick Books, 2002.

Payne, Blanche, Geitel Winakor, and Jane Farrell-Beck. *The History of Costume.* 2nd ed. New York: HarperCollins, 1992.

Ruby, Jennifer. *The Stuarts: Costume in Context.* London, England: B. T. Batsford, 1988.

Baldric

A baldric was a broad belt that was not worn around the waist. Instead, it was strapped over the shoulder; it extended diagonally across the chest, usually from the right shoulder to the left hip. Baldrics were essential attire for soldiers or anyone else who carried swords, which in the seventeenth century was nearly every gentleman. Baldrics were worn on top of the doublet, but usually under any jacket or cloak. They were the equivalent of a gun's holster, in that they featured an attachment which held the sword in place at the wearer's hip.

Baldrics date back to the time of the Roman Empire (27 B.C.E.–476 C.E.) and were standard gear for most European armies from the fourteenth through the seventeenth centuries. A practical baldric was made of leather, but those owned by wealthier gentlemen in the seventeenth century were often decorated with jewelry or featured gold trimming. Men might also wear decorations on baldrics to indicate membership in a military unit. When the baldric was worn without a sword it was generally called a sash.

Across the centuries, baldrics made of cloth were worn by civilians and used to carry bags. They also were worn by members of marching bands, whose instruments were attached to them as they walked in parades. Baldrics have also been used for ceremonial purposes. For example, the drum major of the United States Military Academy band wears a special baldric that is lined with red trimming and features a crossed drumsticks logo, reflecting the fact that the first American soldier-musicians were drummers.

FOR MORE INFORMATION

Cohen, Richard A. *By the Sword: A History of Gladiators, Musketeers, Samurai, Swashbucklers, and Olympic Champions.* New York: Random House, 2002.

Oakeshott, R. Ewart. *A Knight and His Weapons.* 2nd ed. Chester Springs, PA: Dufour Editions, 1997.

Breeches

Breeches remained the most common form of legwear for men in the seventeenth century. There were important changes to breeches in the seventeenth century that brought them closer to the trousers commonly worn today.

For the first few decades of the century breeches remained as they were in the previous century—baggy, puffy pants that were often given shape with padding known as bombast. By the 1620s, however, men began to discard the padding and wore much slimmer fitting breeches that came to the knee. The breeches were fastened at the knee with a garter, ribbon, or buttons, and at the waist with a button or drawstring. Hose or stockings covered the lower half of men's legs.

These closer-fitting breeches allowed for easy movement and gave men the tall, slim profile that became fashionable in the middle part of the century. As coats, vests, and justaucorps grew longer, however, the breeches were seldom seen. In later centuries breeches would grow longer, eventually extending all the way to the ankle and becoming modern trousers and pants.

A strange version of the breeches that became popular in the 1660s were called petticoat breeches. Baggy like the trunk hose and pumpkin breeches of an earlier era, these breeches were puffed out to look like a skirt worn with petticoats. Men quickly discarded this fashion in favor of normal breeches, which could be made of a variety of fabrics, from wool to silk.

FOR MORE INFORMATION

Davis, R.I.; additional material by William-Alan Landes. *Men's 17th & 18th Century Costume, Cut & Fashion: Patterns for Men's Costumes.* Studio City, CA: Players Press, 2000.

Hart, Avril, and Susan North. *Fashion in Detail: From the 17th and 18th Centuries.* New York: Rizzoli, 1998.

Payne, Blanche, Geitel Winakor, and Jane Farrell-Beck. *The History of Costume.* 2nd ed. New York: HarperCollins, 1992.

Bustle

Women wore bustles underneath the backs of their skirts for several centuries beginning in the sixteenth. Bustles consisted of various objects, including cushions, pads, and frames made of wire and wood, that were tied around the waist or directly attached to a woman's skirts. The purpose of the bustle was to add fullness or shape to the skirt, and it was often used in combination with farthingales, which were stiff hoops, or petticoats, that were worn as full underskirts.

The design and filling of bustles, and the manner in which they were worn, changed from century to century, and even from decade to decade. Bustle types related directly to the kinds of dresses currently in style. They were much needed with the full skirts of the sixteenth and seventeenth century, and were used along with farthingales. But when slimmer dress profiles of the mid-seventeenth century were in fashion, bustles were not needed. This cycle occurred again in the nineteenth century. In the 1870s bustles were out of

The purpose of the bustle, worn underneath the back of the skirt, was to add fullness or shape, and it was often used in combination with farthingales, stiff hooped underskirts. *Reproduced by permission of © Historical Picture Archive/CORBIS.*

fashion because women were wearing dresses made of smaller amounts of cloth. Fuller dress styles were introduced in Paris in 1880 and London three years later. The bustle that accompanied them was made of a cushion filled with straw, which was sewn directly into the dress. This bustle also included a number of steel half-hoops placed in the dress lining, which thrust out the dress behind the waist.

From the late nineteenth century on, bustles were occasionally worn only with ball gowns. For the most part, however, they have been out of style throughout the twentieth century and into the twenty-first century.

FOR MORE INFORMATION

Cunnington, C. Willett, and Phillis Cunnington. *Handbook of English Costume in the Seventeenth Century.* Boston, MA: Plays, Inc., 1972.

Payne, Blanche, Geitel Winakor, and Jane Farrell-Beck. *The History of Costume.* 2nd ed. New York: HarperCollins, 1992.

[*See also* **Volume 3, Sixteenth Century: Farthingales; Volume 3, Seventeenth Century: Petticoats**]

Falling and Standing Bands

Neckwear was an important component of dress for both men and women in the sixteenth and seventeenth centuries, and they devised many ways to decorate the neck. Most popular in the sixteenth century were the ruff, a stiffly frilled collar that encircled the neck, and the whisk, a wide fanned collar around the back of the neck. By the mid-seventeenth century, when clothing styles were more subtle and understated, the band was more popular and it came in two primary styles: the standing band and the falling band.

Both bands were forms of collars and were either part of a shirt or bodice, or attached to the shirt or bodice with small ties. A band was tied at the neck with band strings, which were finished out with small tassels or decorative knots or balls. The standing band was stiffened with starch and stood up and flared away from the neck at the sides and back; it was open in front. The standing

The falling band was a neck decoration made of silk or linen that fastened at the neck and was draped over the shoulders, chest, and back. *Painting by Karel van Mander. Reproduced by permission of © Archivo Iconografico, S.A./CORBIS.*

band could be as narrow as two inches or, at its most extravagant, as wide as a foot. Many standing bands were trimmed with lace, which remained popular through the century. The larger standing bands were similar to the whisks or golillas worn earlier in the century.

The falling band was more subtle than the standing band. Made of unstiffened silk or cambric, a fine white linen, it fastened at the neck and draped over the shoulders and down the chest and back. Falling bands could extend as far as the edge of the shoulder and might be either very plain, if worn by a Puritan (strictly religious person against excess in personal display), or elaborately trimmed with lace, if worn by a Cavalier (Catholics who favored ornamentation).

FOR MORE INFORMATION

Payne, Blanche, Geitel Winakor, and Jane Farrell-Beck. *The History of Costume.* 2nd ed. New York: HarperCollins, 1992.

Yarwood, Doreen. *The Encyclopedia of World Costume.* New York: Charles Scribner's Sons, 1978.

[*See also* **Volume 3, Sixteenth Century: Ruffs; Volume 3, Sixteenth Century: Medici Collar box on p. 484; Volume 3, Seventeenth Century: Whisk**]

Gowns

The primary garment worn by women of all social classes was the gown, consisting of a close-fitting bodice with attached decorative sleeves and full skirts. Though the basic form of the garment was very similar to gowns worn during the sixteenth century, a variety of changes made seventeenth-century garments quite distinct. Perhaps most notable were changes in the way skirts were worn.

The gown of the early seventeenth century continued the fashions of the sixteenth century. Skirts were given their shape by stiff farthingales, or underskirt hoops, and bodices were stiffened with flat stomachers. Sleeves were puffy and full, completely covering the arms. Beginning in about the 1620s the styles began to change quite noticeably. The first change, a shortening of the sleeves to reveal a woman's wrists, marked the first time women's arms were visible in the hundreds of years of European costume history. Soon women's arms could be bared up to the elbow. Often, however, more modest women would wear an undershirt with long lacy sleeves that came over the wrist.

The 1630s saw a general softening of the outline of women's gowns. Stomachers became less rigid and the bodice was allowed to follow the natural contours of the body. Skirts became less rigid as well, as farthingales went out of favor in every European country except Spain, where they remained in use. Underneath the top skirt women now wore petticoats, sometimes several petticoats, to give the skirt shape.

Fashions changed once more after the 1650s. Stomachers grew stiffer and flatter once again, and they also lengthened and came to a point below the line of the waist. As with men's costume, women's gowns sought to give the wearer a thin, elongated profile. Perhaps the most important changes had to do with skirts. Overskirts began to be parted to reveal decorative petticoats. In a popular style called a mantua, or manteau, the overskirt was pulled up at the front and sides and fastened in flowing billows or bunches, revealing a decorative petticoat. The outer skirt of the mantua was often worn very long to form a train, a length of skirt that trails on the ground. Another popular late-century style was the décolleté neckline, a low cut neckline which revealed the upper part of a woman's breasts. More modest women, as always, tended to cover this area with a scarf or a light undershirt.

Women of all classes wore gowns, though there were wide differences in materials and the complexity of the tailoring. Among the wealthy satin was the most popular fabric, followed by velvet and rich brocade. These fabrics were often carefully embroidered, though they were never as ornate and ornamented as in the sixteenth century. Poorer women might wear gowns made of wool or cotton. The tailoring of their garments was much simpler. While a rich woman's bodice might be made of a dozen different panels, a poor woman's was made of just a few. And while a rich woman might wear five to ten rustling petticoats, a poor woman might wear no petticoat at all beneath her overskirt.

FOR MORE INFORMATION

Bigelow, Marybelle S. *Fashion in History: Apparel in the Western World.* Minneapolis, MN: Burgess Publishing, 1970.

Cassin-Scott, Jack. *Costume and Fashion in Colour, 1550–1760.* Introduction by Ruth M. Green. Dorset, England: Blandford Press, 1975.

Hatt, Christine. *Clothes of the Early Modern World.* Columbus, OH: Peter Bedrick Books, 2002.

Payne, Blanche, Geitel Winakor, and Jane Farrell-Beck. *The History of Costume.* 2nd ed. New York: HarperCollins, 1992.

[*See also* **Volume 3, Sixteenth Century: Gowns; Volume 3, Seventeenth Century: Stomacher**]

Justaucorps

A long coat worn over a shirt and vest, the justaucorps was one of the most common overgarments worn by men during the seventeenth century. It was also an important garment in the history of men's coats, for it marked an important stage in the long transition from the form-fitting doublet of the fifteenth century to the loosely fitting frock coat of the nineteenth century.

By the mid-seventeenth century people across Europe were breaking from the stiffness and excessive ornamentation of sixteenth-century fashion and seeking more comfortable garments with longer, more elegant lines. Men began to wear a long garment, based on the doublet, that fit closely in the shoulders and sleeves, but flared outward at the waist and hips. Gradually this collarless garment, called a justaucorps (or justacorps), reached all the way to the calves. The lower part of the garment, called the skirt, might consist of several panels that flared outward over the breeches. The justaucorps was often fastened only at the neck, and gaped open in an inverted V shape.

The justaucorps was a flexible garment that was altered to fit the fashions of the day. It might have embroidered designs at the hem and the sides, and could be made of either plain wool or sumptuous velvet or silk to suit the wearer's tastes. By the eighteenth century the justaucorps featured wide cuffs and stiffened skirts. Eventually the justaucorps would transform into the collared frock coat, the precursor to the modern suit coat.

FOR MORE INFORMATION

Bigelow, Marybelle S. *Fashion in History: Apparel in the Western World.* Minneapolis, MN: Burgess Publishing, 1970.

Payne, Blanche, Geitel Winakor, and Jane Farrell-Beck. *The History of Costume.* 2nd ed. New York: HarperCollins, 1992.

[*See also* **Volume 3, Fifteenth Century: Doublet; Volume 3, Eighteenth Century: Coats and Capes; Volume 3, Nineteenth Century: Coats**]

A long coat worn over a shirt and vest, the justaucorps was one of the most common overgarments worn by men during the seventeenth century. *Reproduced by permission of © Historical Picture Archive/CORBIS.*

Petticoats

Petticoats were full skirts that women wore beneath another skirt beginning in the fifteenth century. There were several reasons for wearing petticoats. One reason was practical: Petticoats added body to the skirt and kept the women who wore them warm. But wearing petticoats was usually done to keep in fashion, especially in the seventeenth century. Once women quit using farthingales, or stiff hoops, to add body to their skirts, they turned to petticoats to do the job. Petticoats worn for warmth were made of wool or cotton, while those worn for fashion were made of taffeta, satin, linen, or a combination of starched fabrics.

Petticoats were full skirts that women wore beneath another skirt to add body to the skirt and for warmth. But wearing petticoats was usually done to keep in fashion, especially in the seventeenth century. *Reproduced by permission of © Historical Picture Archive/CORBIS.*

Petticoats were gathered at the waist and flared outward at the hem. Many were highly ornamental, featuring layers of ruffles, trimming, and lace. Most of the trimming was along the bottom edges, the part most likely to be seen. Beginning in the late seventeenth century women pulled up their outer skirts in a style known as mantua, allowing the petticoats to be seen.

Petticoats were first fashionable to see in the seventeenth century, and then they were mostly an underskirt. After the mid-eighteenth century, petticoats were primarily thought of as a form of underwear. They did come back into fashion in the 1950s and were worn under knee- or calf-length skirts to give them volume. In the 2000s, they are occasionally worn for specific occasions, such as square dances.

Some men in the mid-seventeenth century wore something called petticoat breeches. These elaborately tailored breeches featured loose legs puffed out in a skirt that hung to the knees, and were sometimes worn with smaller petticoat skirts around the calves. This strange style was not around for long.

FOR MORE INFORMATION

Cunnington, C. Willett, and Phillis Cunnington. *Handbook of English Costume in the Seventeenth Century.* Boston, MA: Plays, Inc., 1972.

Yarwood, Doreen. *The Encyclopedia of World Costume.* New York: Charles Scribner's Sons, 1978.

Stomacher

The stomacher was an essential part of women's gowns, from about 1570 to 1770. In its most basic form it was a long V- or

U-shaped panel that decorated the front of a woman's bodice, extending from her neckline down to her waist. (Men sometimes also wore a stomacher with their doublets, though this was less common.) The stomacher could either be part of the bodice or a separate garment that fastened to the bodice with ties. The stomacher had two main purposes: to add decoration and to provide structure. Both decoration and structure changed with passing fashions over the long history of this garment.

During the late sixteenth century stomachers were stiffened with wooden slats or whalebone supports to create the stiff, flat-chested profile preferred at the time. The stiffness of the stomacher matched well with the structure provided by the rigid farthingales holding out women's skirts. By the early seventeenth century the rigidity had been removed from women's gowns, and both stomachers and skirts were softer and more flowing. When fashion shifted again in the late seventeenth century the stiffness returned, though the stomacher now was shaped so as to push the breasts upward in the revealing ways preferred in that age. The rigid shaping effects of the stomacher were later accomplished by the corset used in the eighteenth and nineteenth centuries.

Stomachers also provided an important decorative element to women's gowns. They were often covered in a fabric that contrasted with the rest of the bodice, or complemented one of the skirts. Stomachers were often adorned with ribbons, bows, lace, or, in the sixteenth century especially, jewels. Heavily decorated stomachers became especially popular in the eighteenth century. One of the most popular styles of that century was the échelle or eschelle, a series of bows tied down the front of the stomacher, decreasing in size from the neck to the waist. This style was introduced by French trendsetter Madame de Pompadour (1721–1764), the mistress of French King Louis XV (1710–1774), and was quickly copied throughout Europe as part of a gown style called robe à la française.

To add decoration and to provide structure, the stomacher was a long V- or U-shaped panel that decorated the front of a woman's bodice, extending from her neckline down to her waist. *Reproduced by permission of © Arte & Immagini srl/CORBIS.*

FOR MORE INFORMATION

Cassin-Scott, Jack. *Costume and Fashion in Colour, 1550–1760.* Introduction by Ruth M. Green. Dorset, England: Blandford Press, 1975.

Payne, Blanche, Geitel Winakor, and Jane Farrell-Beck. *The History of Costume.* 2nd ed. New York: HarperCollins, 1992.

Yarwood, Doreen. *The Encyclopedia of World Costume.* New York: Charles Scribner's Sons, 1978.

[*See also* Volume 3, Sixteenth Century: Gowns; Volume 3, Seventeenth Century: Gowns; Volume 3, Eighteenth Century: Corsets; Volume 3, Eighteenth Century: Robe à la Française]

This man wears a vibrant red waistcoat. From the sixteenth through the eighteenth centuries, men's waistcoats were long-sleeved garments worn as middle layers of clothing, over a shirt but underneath a topcoat or justaucorps. *Reproduced by permission of © Gianni Dagli Orti/CORBIS.*

■ ■ ■ Waistcoat

The waistcoat has been one of the standard pieces of formal dress in the West since the late sixteenth century, and it has gone through several changes over time. From the sixteenth through the eighteenth centuries, men's waistcoats were long-sleeved garments worn as middle layers of clothing, over a shirt but underneath a topcoat or justaucorps. Some men's waistcoats extended only to the waist, hence their name, while others continued several inches lower. Generally, they grew shorter as time passed. Waistcoats were buttoned down the front, and featured collars and pockets. By the eighteenth century, a man's formal suit consisted of a coat, waistcoat, and breeches, or pants.

Women also sometimes wore waistcoats between their outerwear and underwear. Some were sleeved but most were sleeveless. Unlike menswear, however, women's waistcoats were considered intimate apparel, and were not meant to be seen by anyone but the wearer. Still, they cannot be classified as underwear. By the eighteenth century, women wore vest-like waistcoats as riding attire and white, snugly sleeved waistcoats as blouses with long skirts.

The first waistcoats for both sexes were usually made of linen. They were padded and textured like quilts and featured ornate silk embroidery, known as whitework. Though they might be highly decorated, the primary purpose of the early waistcoats was to keep the wearer warm.

In the twentieth century, the waistcoat took on a new meaning as the equivalent of a vest. Different styles are worn for different purposes. Some are luxury designer items that are embroidered or even hand-painted, and donned for dressy occasions. Others are lined and sturdily made, and are worn for such outdoor activities as hunting and fishing or simply when it is too warm to wear a jacket or coat but not hot enough to be outdoors without some form of outerwear.

FOR MORE INFORMATION

Bigelow, Marybelle S. *Fashion in History: Apparel in the Western World.* Minneapolis, MN: Burgess Publishing, 1970.

Hart, Avril, and Susan North. *Fashion in Detail: From the 17th and 18th Centuries.* New York: Rizzoli, 1998.

Payne, Blanche, Geitel Winakor, and Jane Farrell-Beck. *The History of Costume.* 2nd ed. New York: HarperCollins, 1992.

Whisk

Related to the standing collar and the ruff, the whisk was an especially stiff and ornate neck decoration worn during the first decades of the seventeenth century. Like many fashion trends of this period, the whisk originated in Spain, and evolved from the golilla. The golilla was a collar of stiffened fabric or cardboard that was trimmed in lace and worn with another fabric collar. Adapted for use in England, Germany, and Flanders (present-day Belgium and Netherlands), the whisk was a wide standing collar that was often held in place by a wire framework and made of ornate lace or scalloped fabric. The whisk was rounded in back of the head and had a straight edge that stood over either shoulder.

Ornate almost to the point of excess, whisks represented the high point of the late-sixteenth and early-seventeenth-century trend toward ornament. They made moving the head uncomfortable, and were often worn with another collar, adding to the difficulty. By midcentury they had been replaced by the more practical standing and falling bands.

FOR MORE INFORMATION

Payne, Blanche, Geitel Winakor, and Jane Farrell-Beck. *The History of Costume.* 2nd ed. New York: HarperCollins, 1992.

Yarwood, Doreen. *The Encyclopedia of World Costume.* New York: Charles Scribner's Sons, 1978.

[*See also* **Volume 3, Seventeenth Century: Falling and Standing Bands**]

Seventeenth-Century Headwear

A well-groomed head was important for both men and women during the seventeenth century. At the beginning of the century fashionable men wore their natural hair quite long with lovelocks, or extra long strands of hair, dangling over their left shoulder. In addition, their faces were tufted with mustaches and beards. Kept neat with wax, men's mustaches and beards ranged from full and thick to pencil-thin lines. But when the hair of the French king Louis XIV (1638–1715) began to fall out in the late 1600s, the king and, subsequently, more and more men began to wear thick, flowing wigs. As the volume of hair on their heads increased, men wore smaller and smaller beards and mustaches, until most were clean-shaven by the end of the century.

At the beginning of the century men wore fancy versions of the copotain hats of the previous century, with high crowns and wide brims, often stuck with large plumes, or feathers. However, the preferred hat by the end of the century was a simple, low-crowned tricorne hat. Rather than elaborate decoration, the angle at which the tricorne sat on a man's head became a fashionable art.

The styles for women's hair changed less dramatically over the course of the century. Curled or frizzed, women's hair was worn swept up into high piles at the beginning of the century, fluffed at the sides during midcentury, and again, at the end of the century, worn quite tall, in towering fontage hairstyles. Jewels, lace, linen,

In the seventeenth century more and more men began to wear thick, flowing wigs. As the volume of hair on their heads increased, men wore smaller and smaller beards and mustaches, until most were clean-shaven by the end of the century. *Courtesy of the Library of Congress.*

and ribbons, as well as occasional masculine-style hats, added to women's hairstyles.

Worn dark brown or black throughout most of the century, the hair of both men and women was heavily powdered by the end of the century, a trend that, with wigs, would dominate the next century.

FOR MORE INFORMATION

Batterberry, Michael, and Ariane Batterberry. *Fashion: The Mirror of History.* New York: Greenwich House, 1977.

Bigelow, Marybelle S. *Fashion in History: Apparel in the Western World.* Minneapolis, MN: Burgess Publishing, 1970.

Corson, Richard. *Fashions in Hair: The First Five Thousand Years.* London, England: Peter Owen, 2001.

Fontange

In 1680 the fontange became the most fashionable women's hairstyle and remained popular until the early eighteenth century. The style was created by the Duchesse de Fontanges, the mistress of the French king Louis XIV (1638–1715), when the hairstyle she was wearing at the time was ruined while out hunting. She hastily gathered her curled hair on top of her head with a ribbon from her outfit. The style enchanted the king and other women began copying the style. At first the style consisted of a small pile of curled hair with ribbons and bows just above the forehead. The fontange eventually grew into a high tower of curls piled over a wire foundation, sometimes with false curls. The style was so often worn with a starched linen frill in the front that the linen cap came to be called a fontange as well. By the end of the century these linen caps were starched and wired to create very tall headdresses.

The height of the fontange related to a general trend in the seventeenth century for fashion to emphasize a vertical line. As the fontange grew taller, women had great difficulty securing it on their heads. Then, when finally secured, the fontange often slipped to one side or another. Women found the instability of the fontange so frustrating that many began suggesting that the heads of infant girls should be flattened to better hold the fontange later in life. No evidence of anyone actually doing this exists and the style fell from fashion in the early eighteenth century.

FOR MORE INFORMATION

Corson, Richard. *Fashions in Hair: The First Five Thousand Years.* London, England: Peter Owen, 2001.

Payne, Blanche, Geitel Winakor, and Jane Farrell-Beck. *The History of Costume.* 2nd ed. New York: HarperCollins, 1992.

■ Hurly-Burly

Originating in Paris, France, the hurly-burly, also known as hurluberlu, became a fashionable hairstyle for women during the Baroque period of the seventeenth century, during which time people favored extravagant fashions. The hurly-burly consisted of shoulder length or shorter curls falling in ringlets from a dramatic center part to frame a woman's face. With its masses of curls, the hurly-burly was a dramatic expression of the many varieties of curls set with gum arabic, a sticky, resin-like substance extracted from African trees in the Acacia family, that were very popular among women at the time.

FOR MORE INFORMATION

Kelly, Francis M., and Randolph Schwabe. *Historic Costume: A Chronicle of Fashion in Western Europe, 1490–1790.* 2nd ed. New York: Charles Scribner's Sons, 1929.

■ Lovelocks

Lovelocks were a small lock of hair that cascaded from the crown of the head down over the left shoulder. Lovelocks were longer than the rest of the hair and were treated as special features. Men, and some women, wore lovelocks curled into a long ringlet, braided, or tied at the end with a ribbon or rosette, a ribbon twisted into the shape of a rose.

Although considered quite fashionable, many people detested lovelocks, considering them unnecessary and extravagant. In 1628 a sixty-three page book denouncing lovelocks was published. The author, William Prynne, railed against the wearing of lovelocks as "Unlovely, Sinfull, Unlawfull, Fantastique, Disolute, Singular, Incendiary, Ruffianly, Graceless, Whorish, Ungodly, Horred [Horrid], Strange, Outlandish, Impudent, Pernicious, Offensive, Ridiculous, Foolish, Childish, Unchristian, Hatefull, Exorbitant, Contemptible, Sloathfull, Unmanly, Depraving, Vaine, and Unseemly," according to Richard Corson in *Fashions in Hair.* Despite the strong opinions of those who did not wear them, love-locks persisted throughout the seventeenth century, especially among young men.

Worn with one point forward, the tricorne hat emerged as the most fashionable hat for men for most of the eighteenth century. *Courtesy of the Library of Congress.*

FOR MORE INFORMATION

Corson, Richard. *Fashions in Hair: The First Five Thousand Years.* London, England: Peter Owen, 2001.

Payne, Blanche, Geitel Winakor, and Jane Farrell-Beck. *The History of Costume.* 2nd ed. New York: HarperCollins, 1992.

Tricorne Hat

Before large wigs became popular for men during the late seventeenth century, low-crowned, large-brimmed, plumed, or feathered, hats were worn. As wigs increased in size, plumes disappeared and the brims of hats were cocked up. When the brim was folded up in three places, the hat became a tricorne, a three-cornered hat. Generally dark in color, tricornes were often edged with a gold braided trim after about 1675. Worn with one point forward, the tricorne hat emerged as the most fashionable hat for men in the late seventeenth and most of the eighteenth century. To be most stylish, men cocked, or tipped, their tricornes to one side or another.

FOR MORE INFORMATION

Cassin-Scott, Jack. *Costume and Fashion in Colour, 1550–1760.* Introduction by Ruth M. Green. Dorset, England: Blandford Press, 1975.

Payne, Blanche, Geitel Winakor, and Jane Farrell-Beck. *The History of Costume.* 2nd ed. New York: HarperCollins, 1992.

Sichel, Marion. *History of Men's Costume.* New York: Chelsea House, 1984.

Wigs

Wigs became a necessity for French courtiers (officers and advisers) in 1643 when sixteen-year-old Louis XIV ascended the throne sporting long curly hair. For all who could not grow their own, long flowing locks were created with wigs. The fashion persisted when, at the age of thirty-five, the king began to lose so much of his own hair that he needed to add false hair to maintain his beloved style. He eventually shaved off all his thinning hair and wore full wigs.

Wigs came in several different styles, but the most popular by the end of the century was the full-bottomed wig, a mass of long curls parted in the center that towered above the head by several inches and hung down past the shoulders. The style was so huge that a satirist of the time referred to a man's face peaking out from his full-bottomed wig as "a small pimple in the midst of a vast sea of hair," according to Richard Corson in *Fashions in Hair.* The full-bottomed wig was the most formal of all wig styles and continued to be worn by clergy and some professionals, such as lawyers, into the following centuries. But many men had several different styles of wigs for different activities, such as rising in the morning, going to church, hunting, and eating at different meals.

Wigs were made of human, horse, and goat hair and worn over shaved heads. They were dressed with fragrant powders made

Wigs came in several different styles, but the most popular by the end of the seventeenth century was the full-bottomed wig, a mass of long curls parted in the center that towered above the head and hung down to or past the shoulders. *Courtesy of the Library of Congress.*

of nutmeg or orrisroot, the root of a sweet-smelling European iris. The hair was sometimes dyed black, brown, or blond. Hair powder would later become so popular that houses were built with powder rooms made solely for the purpose of dressing the hair.

Although quite popular by the end of the century, wigs were not worn by every man because of their expense. Wigs became a true symbol to differentiate the upper from the lower classes. They were so expensive that some men left them to their heirs upon their own death. The history of the century is also filled with accounts of wig theft. The exclusivity of wigs did not last, however. Wigs became the defining hair accessory of the eighteenth century and were worn by every class of man. While women also wore wigs during the seventeenth century, their styles did not reach the magnitude of men's full-bottomed wigs. It was the next century that saw women wearing huge mountains of false curls.

FOR MORE INFORMATION

Bigelow, Marybelle S. *Fashion in History: Apparel in the Western World.* Minneapolis, MN: Burgess Publishing, 1970.

Contini, Mila. *Fashion: From Ancient Egypt to the Present Day.* Edited by James Laver. New York: Odyssey Press, 1965.

Corson, Richard. *Fashions in Hair: The First Five Thousand Years.* London, England: Peter Owen, 2001.

Trasko, Mary. *Daring Do's: A History of Extraordinary Hair.* New York: Flammarion, 1994.

Seventeenth-Century Body Decorations

While the sixteenth century was an age of excess in ornamentation, the seventeenth century is often thought of as an age of elegance, with greater care for the manner of display than for its abundance. Nowhere is this contrast more evident than in the use of jewelry. While people displayed their wealth in the sixteenth century by sprinkling jewels across their garments, hair, and bodies, people in the seventeenth century were more likely to wear just a few well-chosen jewels to demonstrate their taste. A string of pearls, a golden crucifix on a chain, simple dangling earrings, or a finely carved ring were the preferred jewels among the nobles of this period.

Instead of jewelry, people in the seventeenth century were especially fond of accessories, which they carried in abundance, worn on a belt at their waist, fastened to their body with ribbons, or simply carried in the hands. For men preferred accessories were gloves, a handkerchief, a sword worn attached to a baldric, or shoulder belt, and a fine walking cane. Women accessorized even more heavily, carrying delicate gloves, a handkerchief, a fan, a parasol in the summer, and perhaps a mask. Both men and women wore face patches and carried muffs to warm their hands in the winter. Each of these accessories could be as simple or as luxurious as a person's budget would allow.

The bathing customs of Europeans remained as they had for several centuries: minimal. People believed that immersing the body

Queen Anne wearing a bead choker. People in the seventeenth century were likely to wear just a few well-chosen jewels to demonstrate their taste, such as a string of pearls or a finely carved ring. *Courtesy of the Library of Congress.*

in water caused disease, so they used dry clothes to rub dirt from their bodies and only occasionally washed. To combat the unpleasant smell of body odor people used a great deal of perfume. It was carried in small bags or metal ornaments called pomander, applied to clothes, or worn directly on the body, and was very popular. Kings and queens and wealthy nobles even might have their own perfume makers.

Lead-based makeup remained in use in the seventeenth century, but doctors were becoming aware of the way it damaged the skin and warned against its overuse. More and more, women took great care to maintain a pale complexion by wearing masks or carrying parasols when they were outdoors to block the sun.

FOR MORE INFORMATION

Contini, Mila. *Fashion: From Ancient Egypt to the Present Day.* Edited by James Laver. New York: Odyssey Press, 1965.

Cosgrave, Bronwyn. *The Complete History of Costume and Fashion: From Ancient Egypt to the Present Day.* New York: Checkmark Books, 2000.

Cunnington, C. Willett, and Phillis Cunnington. *Handbook of English Costume in the Seventeenth Century.* Boston, MA: Plays, Inc., 1972.

Canes

The cane emerged as an important fashion accessory for men during the seventeenth century and was every bit as important in a carefully dressed man's wardrobe as gloves and a hat. Although people had carried rough walking sticks or simple canes for centuries, it was during this period that these sticks became carefully crafted items carried by every gentleman. While the most common material for the body of the cane was a wooden shaft, the tops and bottoms of the cane were where a man could distinguish himself. Cane bottoms, or tips, were usually wrapped in metal, and gold or silver was not out of the question for the richest people. Cane tops, or heads, could be topped in gold, silver, amber, imported ivory, or other luxurious and durable materials. These handles could be as simple as a round ball or they could be intricately shaped and carved. Some men wrapped a length of decorative ribbon or a tasseled string around the head of their cane, both as decoration and as a way to hold the cane to the wrist. Canes and other walking sticks remained popular into the twentieth century.

FOR MORE INFORMATION

Cassin-Scott, Jack. *Costume and Fashion in Colour, 1550–1760.* Introduction by Ruth M. Green. Dorset, England: Blandford Press, 1975.

Ruby, Jennifer. *The Stuarts: Costume in Context.* London, England: B. T. Batsford, 1988.

[*See also* **Volume 3, Eighteenth Century:** **Walking Sticks**]

Cravats

Although people had carried rough walking sticks or simple canes for centuries, it was during the seventeenth century that these sticks, often topped with ivory, as seen here, or jewels, became carefully crafted items carried by every gentleman. *Courtesy of the Library of Congress.*

The cravat, introduced in the mid-seventeenth century, is the ancestor of the modern necktie. A long strip of cloth wrapped loosely around the neck, the cravat was one of several items to replace the stiff ruffs worn around the neck in the sixteenth and early seventeenth centuries. Legend has it that the origins of the cravat lie with an army regiment from Croatia, a country in eastern Europe, that was fighting with the French during the Thirty Years' War (1618–48). The soldiers in this regiment wrapped a long scarf loosely around their necks, supposedly to protect themselves from sword blows. When the Croatian soldiers visited Paris the French were captivated by their neckwear and began to adopt it for their own use.

Early cravats were made of the lace that was used so much in the period, but people soon grew to prefer the softer feel of a linen or muslin (sheer cotton fabric) cravat. They developed intricate ways to fold and knot their cravats. A new style of wearing the cravat was invented in 1692 by French soldiers fighting in the Battle of Steinkirk. Too rushed to tie their cravats in an intricate knot, they simply twisted the ends of the cloth and stuck it through a buttonhole

in their waistcoat or justaucorps. This style became known as the steinkirk cravat.

The soft and easy-to-tie cravat was a big improvement on the stiff lace ruffs and bands of the past, and it was worn by both men and women into the nineteenth century, when it was adapted into the modern necktie.

FOR MORE INFORMATION

Bigelow, Marybelle S. *Fashion in History: Apparel in the Western World.* Minneapolis, MN: Burgess Publishing, 1970.

Cosgrave, Bronwyn. *The Complete History of Costume and Fashion: From Ancient Egypt to the Present Day.* New York: Checkmark Books, 2000.

Ruby, Jennifer. *The Stuarts: Costume in Context.* London, England: B. T. Batsford, 1988.

A long strip of cloth wrapped loosely around the neck, the cravat was one of several items to replace the stiff ruffs worn around the neck in the sixteenth and early seventeenth centuries.
Reproduced by permission of © Bettmann/CORBIS.

Earstrings

One of the most unique jewelry innovations of the seventeenth century was the earstring. Both men and women wore earrings during this period, and many added an earstring as well. The most common earstring was a long piece of silk thread, decorated at the ends with rosettes made of ribbon. The earstring was strung through a pierced hole in the ear and the lower rosette was attached. It could hang down below the earrings themselves, adding extra decoration. The earstring often adorned only one side of the head, most commonly the left. It was a sort of detachable lovelock.

Like the earring itself, the earstring has been endlessly adaptable. Earstrings made of very fine metal thread or even of very small chains have been worn in the West ever since their introduction. In the twentieth century it was possible to purchase earstrings with fasteners for small charms, much like a charm bracelet.

FOR MORE INFORMATION

Bigelow, Marybelle S. *Fashion in History: Apparel in the Western World.* Minneapolis, MN: Burgess Publishing, 1970.

[*See also* **Volume 3, Seventeenth Century: Lovelocks**]

Fans

Perhaps the most important accessory for wealthy women in the seventeenth century was the folding fan. Made of fine materials such as silk or decorated paper, stretched between handles of ivory, carved wood, or even fine gold, and studded with jewels, fans were an item used to display the user's wealth and distinction. Women carried their fans dangling from decorative ties at their waist or held them in the hand. Late in the seventeenth century and through the eighteenth century fans became a prime prop in women's social performance. Women coyly hid their faces behind fans, waving them delicately in the air, in the flirtatious courtship rituals of the period. "There was an art in using a fan," writes fashion historian Ruth M. Green, "and some ladies wielded it with such self-conscious stylishness that they provoked the satirists," who ridiculed the exaggerated manners of some fan wavers.

Perhaps the most important accessory for wealthy women in the seventeenth century was the fan, which was often made from feathers. *Courtesy of the Library of Congress.*

Ætatis suæ 21 Aº.1616.

FOR MORE INFORMATION

Cassin-Scott, Jack. *Costume and Fashion in Colour, 1550–1760.* Introduction by Ruth M. Green. Dorset, England: Blandford Press, 1975.

De Vere Green, Bertha. *Fans Over the Ages: A Collector's Guide.* New York: A. S. Barnes, 1979.

[*See also* **Volume 3, Sixteenth Century: Fans**]

Masks

Often considered one of the strangest accessories, masks had both practical and decorative uses among European women. Masks were first worn during the sixteenth century to provide protection from the sun and other elements while women were outside or riding horses, thus preserving the pale complexion that was in fashion. This practical usage of masks continued through the seventeenth and eighteenth centuries, and such masks covered either the full face or just the nose and eyes. Full face masks were made of fine stiffened white cloth with holes for the eyes and mouth. They were held to the head with ties or, in a strange arrangement, with a button that was clenched between the front teeth.

Fashionable half-masks were most popular during the seventeenth century. These masks covered the area around the nose and eyes, and were either held to the head with ties or fastened to a small stick, which required that women hold the mask up to the face in order to remain concealed. Such masks allowed women to conceal their identity while attending the many theater performances that were prohibited for respectable women, or simply to maintain an air of mystery at a party or ball. They were either black or white and were made of silk, satin, velvet, or some other soft material. By the nineteenth century masks had gone out of fashion and were only worn by bandits and people attending masquerades, or costume balls.

FOR MORE INFORMATION

Bigelow, Marybelle S. *Fashion in History: Apparel in the Western World.* Minneapolis, MN: Burgess Publishing, 1970.

Cassin-Scott, Jack. *Costume and Fashion in Colour, 1550–1760.* Introduction by Ruth M. Green. Dorset, England: Blandford Press, 1975.

Muffs

Heating the castles and great halls of wealthy people in the seventeenth century was not easy, especially in the cooler countries in the north, such as England and Scotland. Stone walls and fireplaces in nearly every room could not keep rooms warm enough when the days grew cold. Though people had many layers of clothing to keep their bodies warm, their hands remained exposed and cold. The solution to the problem of cold hands, which seems to have gotten worse during the seventeenth century, when climatic change brought years of very cold winters, inspired the creation of the muff, an insulated tube of fabric or fur into which the hands could be tucked.

Though muffs served a practical purpose, they soon were turned into stylish ac-

Initially created to combat the long, cold winters, muffs, like the checkered one here, were insulated tubes of fabric or fur into which the hands could be tucked. Muffs soon turned into stylish accessories. *Reproduced by permission of © Historical Picture Archive/CORBIS.*

cessories by those wealthy enough to afford them. Light muffs might be made of double layers of satin or velvet, stuffed to provide insulation. Fur soon became the preferred material for muffs. People choose the softest, finest fur for their muffs, which might be decorated with jewels or lace trim. King Louis XIV of France, who ruled from 1643 to 1715, had muffs made from the fur of tigers, panthers, otters, and beavers. Muffs could be fastened to a belt at the waist and secured by a loop of ribbon which hung about the neck.

Muffs continued to be used by both men and women through the eighteenth century. During the eighteenth century, muffs provided a portable home for carrying the small pets that became a brief fashion craze among the very wealthy. After the eighteenth century muffs became exclusively a woman's accessory and are still used for warmth to this day, although more rarely than gloves or mittens.

FOR MORE INFORMATION

Bigelow, Marybelle S. *Fashion in History: Apparel in the Western World.* Minneapolis, MN: Burgess Publishing, 1970.

Cunnington, C. Willett, and Phillis Cunnington. *Handbook of English Costume in the Seventeenth Century.* Boston, MA: Plays, Inc., 1972.

Yarwood, Doreen. *The Encyclopedia of World Costume.* New York: Charles Scribner's Sons, 1978.

Patches

While the placing of false beauty marks, or patches, on the face began in ancient Rome around the first century C.E., it became a widespread fad across Europe from the late 1500s through the 1600s. A dark mole that occurs naturally on the face is sometimes called a beauty mark. Beginning in the late sixteenth century, fashionable men and women imitated this natural mark by sticking black beauty patches on their faces. These patches were eventually used to send signals to members of the opposite sex in flirtatious courtship rituals, but they had a practical use as well. Carefully shaped black patches could be applied to hide blemishes and scars on the face, especially the deep round scars left on those who survived the frequent outbreaks of smallpox. Smallpox was a contagious and often fatal disease that caused its victims to break out in sores. It was the vaccination for smallpox, discovered in 1796, that led to the end of the fashion of wearing beauty patches.

The use of patches as a fashion statement began in Paris, where young women and men began wearing patches made of black taffeta, velvet, silk, or thin leather, cut into tiny circles, crescents, stars, and hearts. These patches were stuck to the face with gum mastic, a type of glue made from the sap of trees. More and more elaborate patch designs were created, in such shapes as sailing ships, horse-drawn carriages, and birds in flight. Small boxes were made so that the fashionable person could carry extra patches, in case one fell off or a new look was desired.

Soon, the patches began to take on meaning and send subtle signals to others at parties and other social events. A patch near the eye indicated passion, for example, and one by the mouth showed boldness. A black spot on the right cheek marked a married woman, while one on the left cheek showed that one was engaged.

FOR MORE INFORMATION

All the Rage. Alexandria, VA: Time-Life Books, 1992.

Bigelow, Marybelle S. *Fashion in History: Apparel in the Western World.* Minneapolis, MN: Burgess Publishing, 1970.

Seventeenth-Century Footwear

People took great care covering their feet during the seventeenth century. Fashionable footwear changed shape during the century, and middle-class and wealthy people eagerly purchased the new shoe styles in order to remain in fashion. Shoes and boots continued to be made on straight lasts, the basic sole pattern, so that a shoe would fit either foot. However, significant changes were made to shoe fastenings, toe shape, sole height, and the decorations applied to the upper, or tops of shoes.

By the end of the sixteenth century, shoes began to change from slip-on styles to more snugly fitting tied styles. During the seventeenth century, shoes began to fasten with ribbons and buckles. The toes of shoes changed from being round to square, and sometimes forked, a style that featured a squared toe with slightly elongated corner points. Square-toed shoes became so associated with men's shoes during the century that, when fashions changed in the next century, an unfashionable man was called "old square toes." All shoes and boots had heels that were at least an inch high, and were more commonly two or three inches high, during the century. Although the shoes of the lower classes and working people were made of durable leather or wool, shoes of the wealthiest people were made with expensive fabrics or delicate leather and elaborate decorations.

During the seventeenth century shoes styles began to split along gender lines. Boots became quite fashionable for men during the century. By the middle of the century, men continued to prefer square-toed shoes, but women started to choose shoes with pointed toes. Some women wore a more elaborate pointed style, called hooked, with a pointed toe that curled upward. Another style reserved for women's shoes was a white rand, a band of leather attaching the upper of the shoe to the sole. Before the seventeenth century, the rand of women's shoes was made of the same color as the sole of the shoe. White rands remained fashionable until the 1760s.

Styles worn by both men and women were slippers, which were heeled slip-on shoes with no upper covering the heel, worn at home or for casual events, and overshoes worn over other shoes to protect them from inclement weather, dirt, and puddles.

FOR MORE INFORMATION

Batterberry, Michael, and Ariane Batterberry. *Fashion: The Mirror of History.* New York: Greenwich House, 1977.

Lawlor, Laurie. *Where Will This Shoe Take You? A Walk Through the History of Footwear.* New York: Walker and Company, 1996.

Pratt, Lucy, and Linda Woolley. *Shoes.* London, England: Victoria and Albert Museum, 1999.

Boots

One of the most important fashion trendsetters during the seventeenth century was the cavalier, or military horseman. Along with his confident swagger, his costume came to mark a certain male style during the century. Noblemen who may never have fought in battle adopted and exaggerated the cavalier's clothes. These cavaliers wore elaborate outfits with large plumed, or feathered, hats and fancy jackets and breeches, or pants. Essential to a cavalier's outfit were large, floppy-topped, high-heeled leather boots. The boots' tops were shaped like a funnel and could reach twenty inches in diameter. The wide tops of their boots could be pulled up over the knee or, more commonly, folded down to mid-calf to display many ruffles of lace-edged linen hose. Commonly boots were dark leather, but some men wore light-colored boots for formal occasions. At the heels of their boots, men wore clinking metal spurs, even at dances. These boot styles were widely copied by men during the century.

FOR MORE INFORMATION

Batterberry, Michael, and Ariane Batterberry. *Fashion: The Mirror of History.* New York: Greenwich House, 1977.

Lawlor, Laurie. *Where Will This Shoe Take You? A Walk Through the History of Footwear.* New York: Walker and Company, 1996.

High-Heeled Shoes

Height was a central feature of seventeenth-century fashion. People accentuated their height with tall hairstyles, long flowing gowns, long straight jackets, and high-heeled shoes. Introduced in the late sixteenth century as a wedged cork heel and adopted from the very high chopine, high-heeled shoes became the dominant style of footwear for both men and women during the seventeenth century.

The heel of seventeenth-century shoes developed into an arched sole with a large square-based heel. At the beginning of the century, heels were quite low, but soon grew to two or three inches in height. By the eighteenth century, some men wore shoes with six-inch heels, which probably made walking without a cane impossible. Heels were made of stacked pieces of leather or blocks of wood. The fanciest shoes covered the heels with the same fabric as the rest of the shoe, but brown leather coverings were most common. The French court of Louis XIV (reigned 1643–1715) popularized red leather heels in the 1650s.

In addition to adding height, high-heeled shoes altered the posture and walk of the wearer. No longer could people stride casually without thought of their feet. Moving gracefully in high-heeled shoes took concentration and practice. High-heeled shoes forced people to thrust their upper bodies forward and take smaller steps. The stiffened posture and delicate movements required by such shoes fit right into the fashion of the times, which valued exaggerated manners. By the next century, children started to learn to walk in high-heeled shoes at an early age.

FOR MORE INFORMATION

Batterberry, Michael, and Ariane Batterberry. *Fashion: The Mirror of History.* New York: Greenwich House, 1977.

Lawlor, Laurie. *Where Will This Shoe Take You? A Walk Through the History of Footwear.* New York: Walker and Company, 1996.

[*See also* Volume 3, Sixteenth Century: Chopines]

European woman ice skating in red ice skates. As ice skating became a popular winter activity in the seventeenth century, skates had evolved from extremely primitive foot coverings to sleekly designed footwear. *Reproduced by permission of © Historical Picture Archive/CORBIS.*

■ Ice Skates

During the seventeenth century, ice skating became a popular winter activity. The idea of gliding across ice had intrigued people for thousands of years, and ice skates had evolved from extremely primitive foot coverings into sleekly designed footwear.

Early skaters tied animal carcasses on their feet to chase oxen and horses across the ice. The oldest surviving ice skates, made of the leg bones of large animals and leather straps, were found in Switzerland and are believed to date from 3000 B.C.E. As one might expect, crude skates made for treacherous skating. In fact, the patron saint of ice skating, St. Lydwina, was a teenaged Dutch girl in 1396 when she was knocked down and fell onto the ice, leaving her an invalid for nearly twenty years. She and her Dutch contemporaries skated on wooden skates with flat iron bottoms, propelling themselves with poles. They developed what became known as the "Dutch roll" type of skating, pushing off of one foot and gliding with the other. French skaters wore wooden shoes with a strip of iron on the soles.

The first major innovation in ice skating occurred in Scotland in 1572, with the invention of thin iron blades for skates. Although the blades required frequent sharpening, these skates glided over the ice in a much more controllable way than earlier flat-bottomed skates. Increased production of skates in the seventeenth century helped facilitate ice skating and speed skating as safe and popular sports activities. All-steel blades, introduced in 1850, did away with the need to sharpen ice skates and further popularized the sport.

FOR MORE INFORMATION

"Speed Skating History." *CNN/Sports Illustrated.* http://www.cnnsi.com/olympics/2002/sport_explainers/speedskating_history (accessed on August 6, 2003).

U.S. Figure Skating Association. *Official Book of Figure Skating: History, Competition, Technique.* New York: Simon and Schuster, 1998.

Shoe Decoration

When shoes with fastenings replaced slip-on styles at the end of the sixteenth century, shoe decoration started to become important. These new shoe styles featured latchets, or straps, that crossed over the top of the foot near the ankle. Latchets had tiny holes into which ribbons were threaded and tied in a bow to hold the shoe snugly in place. With the emphasis on elegant ornamentation in the seventeenth century, shoe decoration became quite ornamental.

Shoe roses became especially popular. Shoe roses were ribbons twisted into a rosette or gathered into a large ruffled puff. These decorations were often made of gold or silver lace-edged ribbons and could be quite expensive. One noted English trendsetter, Richard Sackville, the third Earl of Dorset, who spent his fortune almost entirely on clothes, counted his shoe roses as

Throughout the last half of the seventeenth century, small buckles were used to fasten shoes. The buckles were either worn alone or were accompanied by large ribbon bows.

separate, special items in his wardrobe and especially his shoe roses made of gold lace.

The idea that shoe ornamentation was unique jewelry for shoes carried throughout the century. When buckles first appeared as latchet fastenings in the mid-1600s, they were considered separate from the shoe. Like shoe roses, buckles could be worn with a number of different shoes. Buckles were most often made of silver. Throughout the last half of the seventeenth century, small buckles fastened shoes alone or were accompanied by large ribbon bows. By the eighteenth century, high-heeled shoes with ever larger, more highly decorated buckles had become the most common shoe for both men and women. This trend lasted until the French Revolution (1789–99), when people donated their expensive buckles to help fund the fighting or took off their buckles to hide their wealth and began wearing shoes with laces.

In addition to the added decorations, shoes' uppers and high heels were often made of or covered in expensive fabrics or dyed leather and beautified with embroidery or appliqued patterns. Brocade, an oriental silk fabric patterned with raised designs of silver and gold thread, was often used for the uppers of shoes. Velvet and kid, the soft leather from young goats, were also popular.

FOR MORE INFORMATION

Batterberry, Michael, and Ariane Batterberry. *Fashion: The Mirror of History.* New York: Greenwich House, 1977.

Contini, Mila. *Fashion: From Ancient Egypt to the Present Day.* Edited by James Laver. New York: Odyssey Press, 1965.

Lawlor, Laurie. *Where Will This Shoe Take You? A Walk Through the History of Footwear.* New York: Walker and Company, 1996.

Eighteenth-Century Revolt

The eighteenth century ushered in sweeping changes to the lives of rich and poor alike. The rural, agriculturally-based economies of Europe began a centuries-long transformation into modern industrially-based economies. The early years of the Industrial Revolution brought technological advances that improved agricultural production and sped up the manufacture of goods, laying the groundwork for the factory system that would soon dominate European countries and the newly formed United States of America. Better transportation between distant places made it possible to buy and sell more goods. England rose to become the most technologically advanced nation in the world and imposed its power across the globe.

The growth of the middle class

At the beginning of the century Europeans were divided into distinct social classes. Noblemen owned vast tracts of land on which peasants labored for very little compensation, while shopkeepers, professionals, and some skilled workers made up a small middle class. However, as trade routes between European countries and distant lands became firmly established, merchants began developing great wealth. With these economic changes wealth was spread among more people. Merchants and factory owners soon had enough wealth to dictate important parts of political and economic life and to influence fashions. No longer were wealthy nobles the only people who could afford the luxuries of life.

Along with more luxurious food, housing, and clothing, the growing middle class began devouring knowledge. A group of intellectuals developed new ideas about politics and human potential. By the end of the century the Age of Enlightenment had become a

In the eighteenth century, English tailors triggered a trend toward well-made, somber-colored clothes for men and more severe fashions for women. *Reproduced by permission of © Gianni Dagli Orti/CORBIS.*

EIGHTEENTH-CENTURY REVOLT ■ ■ ■

popular cultural movement that favored reason over authority. Intellectuals questioned the leadership of royalty and the church and supported free thought. The French philosophers Voltaire (1694–1778) and Jean-Jacques Rousseau (1712–1778) laid the foundations for the civil unrest that led to the French Revolution (1789–99) with such revolutionary ideas as "man is born free, and is every-where in chains," as Rousseau wrote in his *Social Contract* in 1762. Their ideas led to the development of the French Republic and to future forms of democracy.

Bloody conflict

The economic and social changes that occurred throughout the eighteenth century were punctuated by several wars and revolutions. At the beginning of the century most of Europe was embroiled in the War of the Spanish Succession (1701–14), in which England, Holland, and other countries stopped the unification of France and Spain to prevent the two countries from having too much power. Europeans fought a number of other wars during the century, but the most dramatic was the French Revolution that started in 1789, which violently toppled the monarchy, or kingdom, of France and dragged much of Europe into a number of conflicts that erupted off and on until 1815. Although the American Revolution (1775–83) charted a new course for the independent American colonies, it did not have as large an impact on European life as the French Revolution during the eighteenth century.

The wars in Europe shifted power on the continent from France to England. By the end of the eighteenth century, France had lost most of its holdings and England controlled the seas, had accumulated many distant possessions, and was the most powerful industrial economy in the world. With its newly won political and economic power, England also became a center for fashion. France had been the trendsetter for fashions up until this point, dictating ever more extravagant fashions that culminated with the Rococo style, or a decorative style of architecture, fashion, and interior design that featured purely ornamental designs and ornament with intricate floral patterns, popular between 1715 and 1775. Now English tailors triggered a trend toward well-made, somber-colored clothes for men and more severe fashions for women. By the end of the century unadorned English clothes once worn for everyday wear had become fashionable enough for royalty to wear. Although the French

EIGHTEENTH-CENTURY REVOLT ■ 553

Revolution impacted fashion choices for a brief period, England's beautifully tailored clothes dominated the end of the century and influenced clothing styles into the next century.

The importance of clothes

The skill of English tailors was not the only factor in the popularity of English clothes during the century. Textiles were by far the largest industry in England, and mechanized looms, or weaving machines, threatened home-based production. Huge quantities of raw cotton imported from America was woven into cloth and sold around the world. New spinning, dyeing, and weaving technologies developed at the end of the century would influence the next century even more. In the eighteenth century good quality fabric was available to more people than ever before. Merchants advertised clothing to the masses. Paper dolls were printed and distributed with paper clothes in the latest fashions. Unprecedented numbers of people bought new fabrics and wore nicely tailored clothes.

FOR MORE INFORMATION

Batterberry, Michael, and Ariane Batterberry. *Fashion: The Mirror of History.* New York: Greenwich House, 1977.

Bigelow, Marybelle S. *Fashion in History: Apparel in the Western World.* Minneapolis, MN: Burgess Publishing, 1970.

Black, Jeremy. *Eighteenth Century Europe, 1700–1789.* New York: St. Martin's Press, 1990.

Contini, Mila. *Fashion: From Ancient Egypt to the Present Day.* Edited by James Laver. New York: Odyssey Press, 1965.

Cosgrave, Bronwyn. *The Complete History of Costume and Fashion: From Ancient Egypt to the Present Day.* New York: Checkmark Books, 2000.

Dunn, John M. *The Enlightenment.* San Diego, CA: Lucent Books, 1999.

Kallen, Stuart A., ed. *The 1700s.* San Diego, CA: Greenhaven Press, 2001.

Eighteenth-Century Clothing

Men and women wore very different clothes at the beginning of the eighteenth century than they did at the end. The skill of tailors and dressmakers had developed to such an extent that clothing styles were lavished with attention to detail and ornament by midcentury. However, despite the growing skills of tailors, dress became simpler by the end of the century. The dramatic changes reflected the political and cultural changes during the century, including the American (1775–83) and French (1789–99) Revolutions. Throughout Europe and the newly created United States of America, people's attitudes about dress changed. No longer were the monarchs the only trendsetters of fashion. Later, toward the end of the century, clothing styles began to simplify as people looked to the country and to nature for fashion inspiration.

At the beginning of the eighteenth century, men wore outfits similar to those worn in the previous century. On their upper bodies wealthy men wore white linen or cotton shirts with a lace-edged jabot, or tie, topped with sleeveless waistcoats and a long-sleeved justaucorps, long overcoats. Below they wore satin knee breeches and silk hose held at the knee with garters. Working men wore much simpler, less well-made clothes of wool or cotton. By the middle of the century, wealthy men wore the same clothing, but the fit and decoration of these styles had changed quite a bit. The skirts of waistcoats stuck out away from the man's hips with padding or boned supports, and knee breeches fit very tightly against the leg. The fabric for men's clothes was bright and often elaborately embroidered with flowers or curving lines. Men's clothes at the end of the century, however, were very different. Most men wore dark clothes with little decoration. With the rejection of decoration, the difference between a working man's clothes and a wealthy man's became noticeable only from the cut and the quality of the fabric.

Women's clothing styles changed just as dramatically as men's. From the beginning to the middle of the century, women's clothing became larger and more laden with decoration. Wealthy women wore dresses made of brightly colored stiff silk woven with bold floral and striped designs, and many chose Chinese fabrics for their dresses. By midcentury the skirts of women's dresses held many yards of decoration, including layers of ruffles, bows, and lace, and were held out away from the hips with the help of panniers, or stiff hoops.

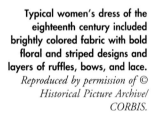

Typical women's dress of the eighteenth century included brightly colored fabric with bold floral and striped designs and layers of ruffles, bows, and lace. *Reproduced by permission of © Historical Picture Archive/ CORBIS.*

In great contrast to the width of their skirts, women's waists were cinched tightly in corsets. The front of their gowns cut deep to display the tops of their breasts and were so revealing that some women tucked lace scarves, called modesty pieces, along their necklines to hide their breasts. Most dresses had three-quarter length sleeves to which women added engageantes, or many tiers of ruffled white lace at the elbow. By the end of the century, however, women discarded these huge and elaborate dresses for the robe en chemise, a simple white cotton dress with a high waist and tiny sleeves.

Before the eighteenth century, children wore smaller versions of adult clothes. But in the mid-eighteenth century, both boys and girls began to wear simple loose cotton dresses. These were the first distinct children's clothes. They were developed due to a change in thought about children's education brought about by two philosophers, John Locke (1632–1704) and Jean-Jacques Rousseau (1712–1778). Locke and Rousseau said that children should be free to play and develop as individuals. Without tight corsets and long coats, children could move more easily. These new ideas took a while to catch on; it wasn't until the early twentieth century that all children were dressed in practical clothing made especially for them.

FOR MORE INFORMATION

Batterberry, Michael, and Ariane Batterberry. *Fashion: The Mirror of History.* New York: Greenwich House, 1977.

Baumgarten, Linda. *Looking at Eighteenth-Century Clothing.* http://www.history.org/history/clothing/intro/clothing.cfm (accessed on August 6, 2003).

Bigelow, Marybelle S. *Fashion in History: Apparel in the Western World.* Minneapolis, MN: Burgess Publishing, 1970.

Contini, Mila. *Fashion: From Ancient Egypt to the Present Day.* Edited by James Laver. New York: Odyssey Press, 1965.

Halls, Zillah. *Men's Costume 1750–1800.* London, England: Her Majesty's Stationery Office, 1973.

Halls, Zillah. *Women's Costume 1750–1800.* London, England: Her Majesty's Stationery Office, 1972.

Metropolitan Museum of Art. *The Age of Napoleon: Costume From Revolution to Empire: 1789–1815.* New York: H. N. Abrams, 1989.

Ribeiro, Aileen. *Fashion in the French Revolution.* New York: Holmes & Meier Publishers, 1988.

Sichel, Marion. *History of Children's Costume.* New York: Chelsea House, 1983.

Chinoiserie

During the eighteenth century Europeans coveted Chinese imports and developed an intense interest in Chinese clothes, porcelain, tea, and other items. These items were known as chinoiserie. Europeans imported thousands of bolts of cloth to make Chinese-style clothing and wall and window coverings. European textile manufacturers learned Chinese dyeing techniques and soon printed cloth with Oriental scenes of pagodas, temples, and other Chinese-inspired objects. In addition, Europeans began dyeing cloth in colors once only seen on imported Chinese fabrics, including a pale golden yellow and a light green, called "Chinese green."

Some clothing styles imitated the Far East. The most popular was the banyan, an informal robe, worn by men at home instead of a justaucorps, or a suit coat. Some styles of banyan looked very similar to the cheongsam worn in early Asian cultures. The robe had a stand-up collar, long sleeves, and its opening crossed over the chest to tie just under the right shoulder. Other banyan styles imitated Indian jackets that buttoned up the front and were called Indian gowns. Banyans were made out of expensive silk or printed cotton. They were so popular in the late eighteenth century that many wealthy men had themselves painted wearing a banyan and cap instead of more formal clothing, which had been the norm for centuries. Other oriental styles and patterns would become popular in future eras, including the 1920s and the 1980s.

FOR MORE INFORMATION

Halls, Zillah. *Men's Costume: 1750–1800.* London, England: Her Majesty's Stationery Office, 1973.

Payne, Blanche, Geitel Winakor, and Jane Farrell-Beck. *The History of Costume.* 2nd ed. New York: HarperCollins, 1992.

[*See also* **Volume 2, Early Asian Cultures: Cheongsam**]

Coats and Capes

Men and women could choose from among numerous different outer garments during the eighteenth century. In general people wore a cape or a coat over their clothes to keep warm or to repel rain.

Women wore a variety of large circular capes or cloaks over their long, full dresses. Made of velvet or taffeta, these outer garments were often decorated with ruffles and ribbons or trimmed with fur. Cloaks often had hoods large enough to cover women's huge hairstyles. These large coverings were worn for formal occasions. Other, less formal coats were also available to women. The spencer was a short-waisted jacket with long, tight-fitting sleeves. The casaquin was a hip-length jacket that fit closely in the front but hung more loosely in the back.

Men had a similar selection of outer garments. The most common outfit for a man included breeches, a waistcoat, and a longer jacket called a justaucorps. At the beginning of the century, the justaucorps was a collarless coat that buttoned in the front and reached the calf, but it gradually shortened to just below the hips by the end of the century. The fit of the justaucorps also changed dramatically over the century. During the early part of the century the skirt, or portion below the waist, flared outward, aided by stiffening provided by whalebone or horsehair. It was similar in profile to women's skirts that were supported with panniers, metal and wooden supports used to hold the skirt out away from the legs. As the century continued justaucorps became more formfitting, with the sleeves and skirt becoming tighter. However, the cuffs of the

At the beginning of the eighteenth century, men wore justaucorps, collarless coats that reached the calf. By the end of the century, the coat was shortened to just below the hips. *Reproduced by permission of © Historical Picture Archive/CORBIS.*

justaucorps became larger by the end of the century. The justaucorps eventually developed into the pourpoint, a jacket with a large collar, by the end of the century.

The justaucorps and the pourpoint were both formal jackets. Some men adopted a more relaxed style during the eighteenth century and began to wear a frock coat. The frock coat had a looser fit and collars. Fastened with buttons in the front, it could be double- or single-breasted, two rows or one row of buttons. English men had worn the more casual frock coat made of plain dark cloth when they were in the country. (Many wealthy English men had large country estates that they visited when they wanted to relax.) The frock coat soon became a very fashionable coat for men, even in towns and cities.

Men also wore heavier outdoor coats and cloaks over the justaucorps. The surtout was a large woolen calf-length coat with a rounded collar. It also could have one or two cape-like collars to protect against the rain. The roquelaure was a large cloak worn on the coldest days. The redingote was a large coat that fit closely along the upper body and had large cuffs and a full skirt. By the end of the century military men and academics were the only men who wore cloaks, while all others wore large coats, such as the redingote.

FOR MORE INFORMATION

Batterberry, Michael, and Ariane Batterberry. *Fashion: The Mirror of History.* New York: Greenwich House, 1977.

Bigelow, Marybelle S. *Fashion in History: Apparel in the Western World.* Minneapolis, MN: Burgess Publishing, 1970.

Cunnington, Phillis. *Costumes of the Seventeenth and Eighteenth Century.* Boston, MA: Plays, 1970.

[*See also* **Volume 3, Seventeenth Century: Justaucorps**]

Corsets

The corset, a tightly fastened body suit designed to push up or flatten a woman's breasts, or to hug her waist until her figure assumed an "hourglass" shape (big on the top and bottom, but slim in the middle), was an essential foundation of fashionable dress for women for over four hundred years. Derived from the French word for body, it has been worn throughout the Western world from the sixteenth century to the present. First introduced in the Spanish and French royal courts of the sixteenth century, corsets were designed to mold women's bodies into the correct shape to fit changing fashions of dress. Corsets were not seen, but they provided the shape a woman needed to wear the latest dresses. Because the needed shape changed so often, corset designs changed as well.

By the eighteenth century corsets had become sophisticated and complex. The clothing worn by wealthy women of this period was highly decorative, made of the best materials. Corsets too were made of lavish materials and often had a concealed pocket into which women would tuck fragrant herbs or small packets of perfume. The shape was similar to a funnel, tapering from chest to waist in a straight line, and stiffened with strips of whalebone. These replaced the wood or metal supports of earlier corsets and were used to shape the body into the figure desired. During the eighteenth century it was fashionable for a woman to show much of her bosom. Corsets were designed to force the breasts up and together into a position known as "rising moons." Most women's figures did not conform to this ideal, however, so the corset put a great deal of strain on the body, tearing the skin, breaking ribs, and in some cases even bruising the internal organs. There are recorded cases where women actually died because their corsets were tied too tight.

In France one of the popular corset styles was the Corps Baleine. It was tight fitting and long-waisted, had over-the-shoulder straps, and was worn over a blouse. Its whalebone supports were so rigid they alarmed many medical professionals of the day. Doctors protested, and by 1773 some women in the royal court were excused from wearing whalebone-stiffened corsets. By the

The corset, a tightly fastened body suit, was designed to push up or flatten a woman's breasts, or to hug her waist until her figure assumed an "hourglass" shape. *Reproduced by permission of © Bettmann/CORBIS.*

Napoleonic Era (1793–1815; so named because it coincided with the rule of Napoleón Bonaparte I [1769–1821], emperor of France), cotton had emerged as the most popular corset fabric. Softer, more natural lines became fashionable, and the painful supports briefly went out of favor. In the nineteenth century, as slim waists and the hourglass figure came back into style, corsets again grew very constrictive. Late in the nineteenth century, however, increasing calls for female independence contributed first to the development of freer, less constrictive corset designs, and finally to the garment's decline. In the twentieth century the primary garments for defining a woman's shape were the brassiere and the girdle, a kind of slimming, elastic underpant. Early in the twenty-first century there was a brief return of the corset's popularity, now worn either alone or on top of a blouse for mainly decorative purposes. This most recent corset interest was merely a fad, however, and was never widely adopted.

FOR MORE INFORMATION

Cosgrave, Bronwyn. *The Complete History of Costume and Fashion: From Ancient Egypt to the Present Day.* New York: Checkmark Books, 2000.

Steele, Valerie. *The Corset: A Cultural History.* New Haven, CT: Yale University Press, 2001.

Waugh, Norah. *Corsets and Crinolines.* London, England: B. T. Batsford, 1954.

[*See also* **Volume 3, Sixteenth Century: Farthingales; Volume 4, 1900–18: Brassiere**]

Engageantes

Up until the end of the eighteenth century, the sleeve of most women's dresses ended near the elbow. From beneath the dress sleeve, the ruffled white sleeve of the cotton undergarment was revealed. The exposed ruffles or bits of lace were called engageantes. Engageantes could be a single layer of ruffle or several tiers of frilly lace gathered around a woman's lower arm. Often the lace on the engageantes matched the lace used on the woman's cap and the tuft of lace she often tucked into her bodice near the bustline of her dress. Engageantes continued Europeans' love affair with lace until the end of the eighteenth century, when dress sleeves were shortened to small shoulder caps.

FOR MORE INFORMATION

Contini, Mila. *Fashion: From Ancient Egypt to the Present Day.* Edited by James Laver. New York: Odyssey Press, 1965.

Cosgrave, Bronwyn. *The Complete History of Costume and Fashion: From Ancient Egypt to the Present Day.* New York: Checkmark Books, 2000.

A grandmother, with engageantes peeking out from her sleeves, and her granddaughter. Engageantes continued Europeans' love affair with lace until the end of the eighteenth century. *Reproduced by permission of © Geoffrey Clements/ CORBIS.*

Fashion *à la Victime*

During the later years of the French Revolution (1789–99) at the end of the eighteenth century, many fashionable young people of the upper and middle classes adopted a style called *à la victime,* or "like the victim." This fashion imitated the look of the thousands of people who were executed by the government during the bloodiest period of the revolution. Sporting scarlet ribbons to symbolize the blood of the dead, and cutting their hair short the way the executioners cut their victims' hair, these young people celebrated the fall of the old government while cheering themselves through a horrifying period in history.

The French Revolution led to sweeping social changes in French society. The luxurious lives of the wealthy had created a great deal of anger among the French poor and middle class. This anger at the nobility exploded in many violent acts during the revolution. Some of these acts, such as the opening of the great prison called the Bastille and attacks on the homes of wealthy nobles, were carried out by mobs of poor people. Other acts, like the "Reign of Terror" and other executions of enemies of the revolution, were carried out by the new government with the support of cheering crowds. The Reign of Terror is the name given to a nine-month period in 1793 and 1794 when over sixteen thousand so-called "enemies of the state" were executed in a public square in Paris, France. These enemies, mostly wealthy nobility and royalty, were killed with a new machine called the guillotine, which executed people quickly and efficiently by dropping a heavy blade to slice off their heads. The wonder at the modern marvel of the new killing machine combined with the fear, rage, and excitement aroused by all the deaths, led to the creation of fashion *à la victime.*

The revolution had brought an end to the excessively ornate fashions of the early to mid-1700s. Gone were the tall powdered wigs and hairdos and brilliant jewelry. Fashionable men and women cut their hair short and ragged, high on their neck in the back with curls falling over their foreheads in the front. This *à la victime* cut imitated the way the executioner sheared off the hair of those who approached the guillotine, so that the blade could cut cleanly through the neck. Women's gowns became simple loose dresses, like the nightgowns and underclothes worn by those who were herded from prison cells into carts bound for the public square and death. Red ribbons became stylish, worn around the neck to indicate the bloodline where the head was cut, or wrapped in an "X" across the breasts and around the arms to represent flowing blood. Both women and men wore small reproductions of the guillotine as jewelry. Ladies' hats were designed to look like the Bastille, a prison that had symbolized the cruelty of the old government. For supporters of the new government, these fashions symbolized the demise of the oppressive old rulers.

Though fashion *à la victime* was mainly for those who wanted to show support for the new government, there were also *bals à la victime,* or "dances of the victim." These were large parties to which only those whose relatives had been guillotined were invited. Guests wore black neckbands and armbands and danced together to mourn their dead by celebrating life. The simple styles of the fashion *à la victime* transformed into the Greek-inspired styles of the late eighteenth century such as the robe en chemise.

FOR MORE INFORMATION

Bigelow, Marybelle S. *Fashion in History: Apparel in the Western World.* Minneapolis, MN: Burgess Publishing, 1970.

Ribeiro, Aileen. *Fashion in the French Revolution.* New York: Holmes & Meier Publishers, 1988.

[*See also* **Volume 3, Eighteenth Century: Robe en Chemise; Volume 3, Eighteenth Century: Titus Cut**]

Knee Breeches

Knee breeches, or knee-length leg coverings, were worn by men and boys alike throughout the eighteenth century. Knee breeches were worn pulled up over the hips and buttoned in the front without need for a belt or other brace at the waist. Later the center button was replaced with a front panel that buttoned up either side. Braces, or suspenders, were also added at the end of the century; buttoned to the inside of the waistband, braces secured the knee breeches with straps over the shoulders.

At the beginning of the century, knee breeches were fastened just below the knee with ribbons and buttons, and the stockings were pulled up over them. After 1735 knee breeches featured ornamental buckles and buttons at the knee and from that time on were worn on top of the stockings to display these buckles or decorative buttons. As the century continued, knee breeches changed from rather ill-fitting baggy breeches to formfitting garments. The most expensive breeches were made of satin, while those made for common people were of thick cotton or wool cloth. Breeches at the beginning and middle of the century were made of richly patterned fabric and had decorative embroidery. By the end of the century, knee breeches became much less adorned, but the quality of the fit and fabric remained very high. Although pantaloons, or ankle-length pants, began to be worn by some, knee breeches remained the most commonly worn pant for men during the eighteenth century.

FOR MORE INFORMATION

Bigelow, Marybelle S. *Fashion in History: Apparel in the Western World.* Minneapolis, MN: Burgess Publishing, 1970.

Laver, James. *Costume and Fashion: A Concise History.* 4th ed. London, England: Thames and Hudson, 2002.

Panniers

The smallness of a woman's waist became a very important fashion element by midcentury. To accentuate the smallness of the waist, the skirts of gowns were stiffened and padded to increase their size. Panniers were metal and wooden supports used to hold the skirt out away from the legs; they looked like baskets fastened around a woman's waist. Panniers expanded skirts to widths as large as five feet, so large that two women could not walk through a doorway at the same time or sit on a couch together. Women's large skirts during the mid-1700s influenced the widening of furniture at the time. Just when panniers had spread skirts to enormous and cumbersome proportions, fashion trends shifted to prefer slimmer silhouettes and panniers dropped out of fashion. However, skirts would later be billowed out and supported by crinolines in the following century, just as they had been supported by farthingales in the sixteenth century.

FOR MORE INFORMATION

Bigelow, Marybelle S. *Fashion in History: Apparel in the Western World.* Minneapolis, MN: Burgess Publishing, 1970.

Contini, Mila. *Fashion: From Ancient Egypt to the Present Day.* Edited by James Laver. New York: Odyssey Press, 1965.

[*See also* **Volume 3, Sixteenth Century: Farthingales; Volume 3, Nineteenth Century: Crinoline**]

Polonaise Style

Polonaise style referred to the arrangement of the overskirt of a dress into three bunched swags to give the hips the impression of width and to display the petticoat underneath. Polonaise style featured ankle-length petticoats that revealed high-heeled walking

Woman wearing a polonaise style dress, which featured an overskirt with three bunched swags that gave the hips the impression of width and displayed the petticoat underneath. *Reproduced by permission of © Historical Picture Archive/CORBIS.*

shoes. The style became quite popular during the eighteenth century as a practical garment for walking because the skirts did not drag along the ground.

FOR MORE INFORMATION

Cosgrave, Bronwyn. *The Complete History of Costume and Fashion: From Ancient Egypt to the Present Day.* New York: Checkmark Books, 2000.

Ribeiro, Aileen. *A Visual History of Costume: The Eighteenth Century.* London, England: B. T. Batsford, 1983.

Robe à la Française

The gown that is most associated with the eighteenth century Rococo style, or a decorative style of architecture, fashion, and interior design that featured purely ornamental designs and ornament with intricate floral patterns, popular between 1715 and 1775, is the robe à la française. Made of rich fabrics and loaded with frilly decoration, the robe à la française was worn by only the most wealthy women. It featured a tight-fitting bodice with a square neckline that revealed a great deal of a woman's upper breasts. The ties along the front of the bodice were hidden beneath a stomacher, or triangular panel, that was richly decorated with bows or ruffles. Tight sleeves covered the arm from the shoulders to the elbows, where many layers of lace and ruffles, called engageantes, circled the lower arm. The back of the dress featured the same floor-length pleats as the sack gown and the related robe à l'anglaise. The outerskirt of the robe à la française was made of a fabric, often satin, that matched the bodice and was left open at the front to reveal a ruffled petticoat. The petticoat, like the stomacher, held many decorations: tiers of ruffles, bows, flowers, lace, and other ornamental touches. The skirts of the robe à la française widened over the course of the century with the support of panniers, or hoops used to give shape to a skirt. At the end of the century these elaborate dresses were discarded in favor of much simpler, straighter styles inspired by ancient Greece.

Made of rich fabrics and loaded with frilly decoration, the robe à la française was worn by only the wealthiest of women. *Reproduced by permission of © Historical Picture Archive/CORBIS.*

FOR MORE INFORMATION

Batterberry, Michael, and Ariane Batterberry. *Fashion: The Mirror of History.* New York: Greenwich House, 1977.

Bigelow, Marybelle S. *Fashion in History: Apparel in the Western World.* Minneapolis, MN: Burgess Publishing, 1970.

Contini, Mila. *Fashion: From Ancient Egypt to the Present Day.* Edited by James Laver. New York: Odyssey Press, 1965.

Cosgrave, Bronwyn. *The Complete History of Costume and Fashion: From Ancient Egypt to the Present Day.* New York: Checkmark Books, 2000.

[*See also* **Volume 3, Seventeenth Century: Stomacher; Volume 3, Eighteenth Century: Panniers; Volume 3, Eighteenth Century: Sack Gown**]

Robe en Chemise

By the end of the eighteenth century, heavy, thickly decorated gowns dropped out of fashion as lighter styles, such as the robe en chemise, became popular. In the 1780s English and French women began to wear sheer white cotton dresses with high waists wrapped with satin sashes. These dresses had simple straight silhouettes inspired by ancient Greek and Roman styles. Although the first of these dresses had elbow-length sleeves, many ruffles, and were worn with petticoats, the relative visibility of the female form beneath these thin gowns shocked the public. Upon seeing a portrait of Marie-Antoinette (1755–1793), who was married to Louis XVI of France (1754–1793), in a robe en chemise in 1783, some Parisians considered her to be without clothes. But fashion soon accepted the gowns, and women began to wear even more revealing versions of the robe en chemise. The neckline dipped low in front and the sleeves came to cover only the shoulders. These dresses remained fashionable into the nineteenth century.

FOR MORE INFORMATION

Lister, Margot. *Costume: An Illustrated Survey from Ancient Times to the Twentieth Century.* London, England: Herbert Jenkins, 1967.

Payne, Blanche, Geitel Winakor, and Jane Farrell-Beck. *The History of Costume.* 2nd ed. New York: HarperCollins, 1992.

[*See also* **Volume 3, Nineteenth Century: Dresses**]

INCROYABLES AND MERVEILLEUSES

The *Incroyables* (the Unbelievables) and the *Merveilleuses* (the Marvelous Ones) were part of a rebellious youth movement that arose during the 1790s, during the French Revolution (1789–99). The revolution had begun a tremendous upheaval in France pitting the poor and the middle class against the wealthy, and the government was very unstable. The *Incroyables* (men) and the *Merveilleuses* (women) were political young people, who were the product of an explosive time in history. They made their political statement by dressing in outlandish fashions that exaggerated and mocked the luxurious styles that had been worn in the court of King Louis XVI (1754–1793), who had recently been executed by the revolutionary government. Though many ridiculed the extreme fashions of the *Incroyables* and the *Merveilleuses* and called them immoral, they did remind people of the time before the revolution, when outrageous fashions had been more than a jest.

In the last decade of the eighteenth century, all of French society began to reflect the enormous changes brought about by the French Revolution. The style of dress changed immediately throughout society. The elaborate and ornate styles that had been popular earlier in the century were seen as part of the hated old system, where the rich could afford expensive adornment while the poor starved. Fine clothes were not only unpopular, they could be dangerous, as thousands of people thought to sympathize with the aristocrats were executed. A new style evolved that borrowed simpler fashions from Britain and ancient Greece, both societies that were seen as more democratic than French society. British country clothing, with its long jackets and leather boots, became widely popular. So did long, flowing tunics and gowns, such as the robe en chemise, that resembled the simple robes worn by ancient Greeks in the birthplace of democracy, or the principles of social equality.

Some young people began to rebel against this serious and repressed atmosphere. They began to wear clothing that was a comic exaggeration of the new styles, making them almost as lavish and ridiculous as the finery that had been worn by the nobility before the revolution. Young men, who were soon given the name *Incroyables,* because they looked incredible, wore a cartoon version of the English country suit. Skintight pants with extremely short vests, often made of flowered fabric, were topped with a jacket made so long its wide flared tails reached the ankles. The coat sleeves were so long that they hid the hands from sight, and the lapels were so large they often stuck out several inches beyond the wearer. The back of the bulky coat was bunched in folds, and the front was cut to look uneven when the jacket was buttoned. The jacket collar stood up high behind the head in back, and a huge cravat, or neck covering, was wrapped so high around the neck that it covered the chin and mouth. *Incroyables* cut their hair raggedly, and it hung long and shaggy on the sides of their heads, in a style called "dog's ears." They wore large, two-cornered hats, carried oversized eyeglasses, and often wore two watches.

The female counterparts of the *Incroyables* were called the *Merveilleuses.* The *Merveilleuses* exaggerated the Greek style, wearing loose gowns made of several yards of fabric so sheer that they were almost transparent. They often increased this "naked" look by dampening the cloth of their dresses to make them cling more closely to the body. Their simple, cropped hair was adorned with plumes of ostrich feathers. Both the *Incroyables* and the *Merveilleuses* wore large amounts of heavy musk perfume, which led some to call them "muscadins."

When the military leader Napoleon Bonaparte (1769–1821) rose to power in France at the beginning of the 1800s, he brought a more severe and simple style of dress, along with less tolerance for the outlandish behavior of rebellious youth, and the humorous styles of the *Incroyables* and the *Merveilleuses* disappeared.

Sack Gown

The sack, or sacque, gown evolved from a very informal dress of the late seventeenth century into a formal dress by the mid-eighteenth century. The sack gown was first a loose, tent-like robe worn in the home or by pregnant women. The volume of the gown came from gathers near the shoulders and along the back. The front of the gown skirt was worn either open in the front to reveal a petticoat or stitched closed from the waist down to the hemline. As the century continued, these gowns became more formal, featuring fitted bodices, long full skirts, and a long box-pleated piece of fabric hanging from neck to ankles along their backs. These dresses were so often depicted in the paintings of French painter Antoine Watteau (1684–1721), the man who created the Rococo painting style that emphasized romantic love, that the pleats in back took his name: Watteau pleats. As the dresses became more fitted through the bodice, the gown came to be known as the robe à l'anglaise. The robe à l'anglaise was especially popular in England (anglaise means English in French) and featured a many-pieced bodice with a low neckline. The sack gown went out of style by the end of the century when Greek inspired dresses, such as the robe en chemise, became popular.

FOR MORE INFORMATION

Bigelow, Marybelle S. *Fashion in History: Apparel in the Western World.* Minneapolis, MN: Burgess Publishing, 1970.

Laver, James. *Costume and Fashion: A Concise History.* 4th ed. London, England: Thames and Hudson, 2002.

Trousers

While the wealthiest male citizens in Europe wore knee breeches in the seventeenth and eighteenth centuries, ankle-length trousers had been workingmen's attire for many years. Before the French Revolution (1789–99), the lives of the rich and poor in

France grew further and further apart. The rich lived luxuriously while the poor lived in filth. To topple the tyranny of the wealthy, an angry mob stormed the Bastille, a prison in Paris, France, in 1789 to start the French Revolution. Among the mob were crowds of working people in trousers. Soon revolutionaries were referred to as *sans-culottes,* which meant without breeches. Trousers came to symbolize the ideas of the revolution, an effort to make French people more equal, and it was not long before men of all classes were wearing long trousers.

Trousers soon replaced breeches as the standard leg wear for men in France and England and later the rest of Europe and the United States. Later in the eighteenth century, dandies, or fashionable young men, in England were wearing neatly tailored trousers with straps under the foot or buttons at the ankle.

FOR MORE INFORMATION

Boucher, François. *20,000 Years of Fashion: The History of Costume and Personal Adornment.* Expanded ed. New York: Harry N. Abrams, 1987.

Perl, Lila. *From Top Hats to Baseball Caps, From Bustles to Blue Jeans: Why We Dress the Way We Do.* New York: Clarion Books, 1990.

Eighteenth-Century Headwear

The hairstyles and headwear worn by women changed dramatically and rather frequently during the eighteenth century. The men's styles, on the other hand, gradually became simpler as the century progressed. Shifting fashions had developed deep roots in Western culture by the end of the eighteenth century, and both men and women had become accustomed to yearly, if not seasonal, shifts in fashion, a trend that continues to this day.

Wigs were indispensable hair accessories for men during this century. The long, curled wigs worn by men during the previous century were abandoned by all except older men or those working in law or politics. Without their huge wigs, men experimented with easier-to-manage styles. Professional or middle-class men wore chin- or shoulder-length bob wigs with curled or frizzed powdered hair. Military men made pigtails tied with black ribbons especially fashionable. A man might wear a pigtail tied from his natural hair or attach a wig with a pigtail. Wigs were offered to men in more styles than ever before. Hair could be left plain but was often heavily coated in powder for formal occasions. In keeping with the simpler hairstyles, men also donned less formal hats. Many discarded their tricorne hats of the previous century in favor of tall-crowned, wide-brimmed hats once only worn in the country.

Hairstyles evolved into the most important fashion accessory for women by midcentury, but by the end of the century hairstyles had diminished in importance compared to hats. Hairstyles changed from masses of curled tresses to enormous, towering styles to very short styles, and then back to longer curled locks. Women styled their hair in a variety of tall styles that featured heaps of powdered curls at the beginning of the century. In general, styles followed the lead of Madame de Pompadour (1721–1764), the mistress of French king Louis XV (1710–1774), who fashioned her hair in many

During the eighteenth century professional or middle-class men wore chin- or shoulder-length bob wigs with curled or frizzed powdered hair. *Reproduced by permission of Getty Images.*

different upswept, curled styles. While gray or white powder continued to be used for most occasions, hair left plain was often dyed a fashionable black hue. By the mid-1700s hairstyles had started to climb higher and wider. Hairdressers created monstrously large styles with the help of false hair, pomatum (a sticky oil used to hold the hair in place), and pads or supports for the hair. These large styles were elaborately adorned with stuffed animals, model ships, jewels, feathers, ribbons, false curls, and other ornament. A variety of hats were made to perch atop these large hairstyles. The pouf, for example, enveloped the massive egg-shaped hairdos. These large hats were replaced with smaller caps and hats as styles diminished in size at the end of the century. Amazingly, the cuts that followed the enormous hairstyles of the mid- to late century were very short cuts, including the Titus cut. Although short hair experienced only a brief popularity before longer styles returned to fashion, the dramatic contrast between the large styles of the midcentury and the shorter styles of the late century marked the beginning of a trend toward quickly changing styles that continues today.

FOR MORE INFORMATION

Corson, Richard. *Fashions in Hair: The First Five Thousand Years.* London, England: Peter Owen, 2001.

Laver, James. *Costume and Fashion: A Concise History.* 4th ed. London, England: Thames and Hudson, 2002.

À la Belle Poule

One of the most fashionable hairstyles of the eighteenth century, À la Belle Poule, commemorated the victory of a French ship

LICE, HUNGER, AND HAIR

During the second half of the eighteenth century much of European and American fashion followed the styles of Paris, France. In France the nobles of the court gathered at Versailles, the palace of the French king. There, they had little to do except gossip and design more and more excessive fashions. Men began to wear tall wigs, made of human hair, horsehair, or goat's hair, that were dressed into complex masses of curls. Women placed a horsehair cushion or a wire frame on their heads, then wrapped their own hair over it and piled it high in enormous decorative hairdos, which sometimes rose several feet above the head. Proud hairdressers gave their creations dramatic names, like coiffeur à l'espoir (hairstyle of hope) or coiffeur de la Liberté (hairstyle of liberty) and often topped them off with huge ornaments, like sailing ships, windmills, and whole gardens of flowers. Both men and women held their styles in place with large amounts of hair pomade made from beef fat and covered the whole thing with powder, usually made from wheat or rice flour, sometimes scented and dyed blue, pink, or violet.

Because most Western cultures of the time considered bathing to be dangerous, thorough cleaning of the body was usually only attempted twice a year, in the spring and in the fall. Therefore, perfumes and pouches of fragrant flower petals were used daily to improve the smell of unwashed bodies. These did not, however, prevent parasites like lice from taking up residence in the scalps of both rich and poor.

Lice are small insects that live in the hair of humans and other animals. While the poor most often simply cut off lice-infested hair, the wealthy had to consider their image. Wealthy men could at least remove their wigs and clean them, often by baking them in the oven. They could also shave the head the wig would conceal, and get rid of lice that way. Women however, often preserved their elaborately designed hairdos for months, and lice and other pests were frequently attracted to the fat and flour used to style the hair. Long-handled silver claws were designed to reach in and scratch the itches caused by the lice living inside the coiffure, or hairstyle, and it was not uncommon to see these scratchers laid out with the silverware for guests to use at fancy dinner parties.

Perhaps one of the most important effects of the lavishly styled hair of the French court was caused by the powder itself. At a time when French peasants could barely afford the cost of a loaf of bread, French noblemen and noblewomen stood in powder rooms covered with protective cloths, while servants dusted their hair with great quantities of flour. Poor people who were already angry about the extravagant lifestyle of the wealthy grew even more resentful over this waste of perfectly good food on simple vanity. In 1789 this anger exploded in the French Revolution (1789–99). The poor turned furiously on the rich, determined to get revenge for all the wrongs that had been done. Elaborate hairstyles were replaced by shorter, more natural styles, no doubt much easier to keep lice-free, and flour was once again only used to make bread.

over an English ship in 1778. À la Belle Poule featured an enormous pile of curled and powdered hair stretched over a frame affixed to the top of a woman's head. The hair was then decorated with an elegant model of the *Belle Poule* ship, including sails and flags.

The style resembled, in size and extravagance, other hairstyles popular among women during the century. Just like the À la Belle Poule, each style had its own unique name. One style was created to represent the first vaccine; another showed the solar system. To create a particular style a woman's long hair was pulled up and over a frame or a bundle of wool or horsehair, and topped with flowers, shrubbery, whole birds or other animals, or small model boats or houses, among other things. The tall, wide masses of hair were meticulously curled, smoothed, frizzed, and powdered. Although the fashionable French queen Marie Antoinette (1755–1793) preferred to wear her own hair, other women added false hair to achieve the desired height or width for their hairstyles. The skill and time needed to create these styles meant that women carefully preserved their styles for several weeks at a time. This practice caused the women to get headaches from having to sleep in awkward positions and also created a perfect environment for lice to grow.

The hairstyles became so large that hairstylists climbed ladders to finish the styles; doorways were heightened to accommodate them; they were banned from the general seating area of theaters because they blocked people's view of the stage; and women were forced to stick their heads out of carriage windows or to sit doubled over because their hair was taller than the carriage roof. These elaborately constructed hairstyles were replaced by the 1790s with less cumbersome masses of curled hair.

FOR MORE INFORMATION

Corson, Richard. *Fashions in Hair: The First Five Thousand Years.* London, England: Peter Owen, 2001.

Laver, James. *Costume and Fashion: A Concise History.* 4th ed. London, England: Thames and Hudson, 2002.

Caps

Small white caps made of linen or cotton and edged with lace were quite popular among women and young girls during the early eighteenth century. Two fashionable styles were a mobcap, which covered the head with a puffed white crown bordered by a lace edge, and a round-eared cap, which curved around the head to cover the ears and was edged with lace or ruffles. Both cap types had long fabric streamers called lappets that were left to hang down the back, tied under the chin, or pinned up on top of the cap. As hairstyles grew bigger throughout the century, caps did not. Rather than covering the whole head, caps became dainty accents pinned to the top of enormous piles of hair, often without lappets.

FOR MORE INFORMATION

Batterberry, Michael, and Ariane Batterberry. *Fashion: The Mirror of History.* New York: Greenwich House, 1977.

Bigelow, Marybelle S. *Fashion in History: Apparel in the Western World.* Minneapolis, MN: Burgess Publishing, 1970.

Ribeiro, Aileen. *A Visual History of Costume: The Eighteenth Century.* London, England: B. T. Batsford, 1983.

Pigtails and Ramillies

The Ramillies wig featured a long pigtail tied with black ribbons at its top and bottom. *Courtesy of the Library of Congress.*

The fashion of wearing large, curled wigs in the eighteenth century was impractical for some men. Soldiers developed a unique style that gave them the appearance of long, flowing, curly hair, but allowed them to be active. The style was the pigtail, or queue. Pigtails could be styled in many different ways. Commonly pigtails hung loose from a black ribbon knotted at the back of the head, but they could also be braided, smeared with tar, or completely hidden beneath a tightly wrapped ribbon or fabric pouch. Although the first military pigtails were fashioned from the wearers' own hair, later styles were made of wigs, called campaign wigs. The Ramillies wig, a version of the campaign wig that became a popular style among soldiers throughout the century, was named after a British victory over the French in 1706 during the War of Spanish Succession (1701–14). The Ramillies wig featured a long pigtail tied with a black tie at the top and another at the bottom of the pigtail. Throughout the eighteenth century, pigtails of all sorts were covered in flour or another white powder to create the white hair so popular during the century.

FOR MORE INFORMATION

Corson, Richard. *Fashions in Hair: The First Five Thousand Years.* London, England: Peter Owen, 2001.

Laver, James. *Costume and Fashion: A Concise History.* 4th ed. London, England: Thames and Hudson, 2002.

Pouf

A pouf was a large hat created to cover the elaborate hairstyles of the eighteenth century. Also called a balloon, parachute, or Lunardi hat (after the Italian aeronaut who was one of the first to ride in a balloon in England in 1784), a pouf was a loose, silk hat that encircled the head and had a wide brim. The crown of the pouf looked like a large balloon. When hairstyles shrank in size, poufs were replaced by smaller hats that fit on the head instead of balancing on top of a huge pile of hair.

FOR MORE INFORMATION

Corson, Richard. *Fashions in Hair: The First Five Thousand Years.* London, England: Peter Owen, 2001.

Laver, James. *Costume and Fashion: A Concise History.* 4th ed. London, England: Thames and Hudson, 2002.

Titus Cut

The large hairstyles worn by women during the eighteenth century came to a dramatic end in 1795 when the Titus cut, a short, layered hairstyle, ushered in a fad for short hair among women. The French Revolution (1789–99), which overthrew the French system of nobility, helped popularize short hair as part of a fad. The short hair was meant to imitate the way the executioner sheared off the hair of those prisoners of the revolution who approached the guillotine so that the blade could cut cleanly through the neck. Short hair styles were worn combed up, away from the neck, and the bare neck was wrapped with a red ribbon to symbolize the sacrifice of the guillotine victims.

As with most fads, the Titus cut did not last long. Within a year the Titus cut was worn as a morning style and then covered with a variety of long wigs for the events of the afternoon and evening. As with clothing styles, by the end of the century people had developed a taste for changing hairstyles. Some women changed the style or color of their hair several times a day with the help of wigs.

FOR MORE INFORMATION

Corson, Richard. *Fashions in Hair: The First Five Thousand Years.* London, England: Peter Owen, 2001.

Laver, James. *Costume and Fashion: A Concise History.* 4th ed. London, England: Thames and Hudson, 2002.

Eighteenth-Century Body Decorations

Many of the body decorations and accessories of the seventeenth century continued into the eighteenth century. Women and some men made their faces pale with white makeup made from lead powder, a corrosive substance that led to health problems for many and death for some. Red cheeks were also quite fashionable. Wealthy people used rouge made of crushed red beetles, called cochineals, on their cheeks. Others dabbed berry juice on their cheeks. In addition, women and some men continued to paste fabric patches on their faces to cover their smallpox scars. Masks also continued to be worn throughout the century. Fancy masks were worn to conceal the identity of the wearer at parties or at the theater; green silk masks protected women's skin from the burning rays of the sun during the summer; and black masks kept women's faces warm in the winter.

One trend in hairstyling changed women's faces in midcentury. The fashion for gray powdered hair created a desire for gray eyebrows. Women shaved their own eyebrows and replaced them with false eyebrows made of gray mouse hair. When women began wearing shorter hairstyles at the end of the century, they grew their own eyebrows back. Men also carefully groomed their eyebrows, and some carried small eyebrow combs made specifically for that purpose.

The pocket watch was a valued accessory for men in the eighteenth century. It was attached to a fob, or a decorative string or chain that led from a clip on the waistband to a watch pocket. *Reproduced by permission of © Bettmann/CORBIS.*

·583

For most of the eighteenth century, fashion dictated that women and men carry several accessories. To be fashionable, women carried things from handkerchiefs, handbags called reticules, gloves, fans, parasols, and hand-warming muffs, to pocket watches. Men carried their own accessories, from canes, leather gloves, and pocket watches, to snuff boxes. The most elaborate use of accessories was adopted by the *Incroyables* (the Unbelievables) and the *Merveilleuses* (the Marvelous Ones), the fashionable young people of the century, particularly from France.

At the end of the century, political changes, especially the French Revolution (1789–99), created new fashion trends. At the time of the revolution, many donated or hid their glittering jewelry and began wearing plainer styles. Neck ribbons were especially popular. Both French citizens and aristocrats wore neck ribbons either in celebration or in mourning for the beheaded victims of the guillotine.

Few people bathed during the eighteenth century because most people believed the oils on their bodies protected them from diseases. The stench of unclean bodies was covered with strong-smelling perfume and nosegays, or small bouquets. Not every part of the body was unscrubbed, however. Both men and women vigorously cleaned their teeth in hopes of obtaining a perfectly white smile. Unfortunately, many used harsh chemicals, including gunpowder, acid, and rough pieces of coral, which ate away their teeth's protective enamel coating. These harsh substances caused many people's teeth to rot and fall out. Fake teeth made of ivory and porcelain became necessary.

Missing teeth caused many people's cheeks to look hollow. To give themselves a healthy full-looking face, many people stuffed plumpers, or cork balls, between their gums and cheeks. Plumpers caused people to speak in a funny way, but so many people used them that the funny way of speaking became fashionable, too.

FOR MORE INFORMATION

Bigelow, Marybelle S. *Fashion in History: Apparel in the Western World.* Minneapolis, MN: Burgess Publishing, 1970.

Kalman, Bobbie. *Eighteenth Century Clothing.* New York: Crabtree Publishing, 1993.

Laver, James. *Costume and Fashion: A Concise History.* 4th ed. London, England: Thames and Hudson, 2002.

Cameo

A cameo is a kind of jewelry produced by artisans, or craftsmen, who engrave a bas-relief, or raised, image on a range of single-colored or multicolored materials. In the eighteenth century cameos were made of onyx, sardonyx, ivory, agate, coral, seashell, lava, and glass. If the substance was multicolored, one color was uncovered and became a background for the image engraved on the second color. During the eighteenth century, cameos came in all sizes and shapes; occasionally they were made of separate materials that were glued together. Cameos often were worn on a velvet ribbon or incorporated into an ornate design as a pendant or a pin.

The images on cameos were far-ranging. There were idealized portraits of women's heads and shoulders, posed in profile. The women pictured had classical features, and their hair was shown in great detail. Occasionally, carvers were commissioned to create cameos of specific women. Popular images on cameos also were flowers, groups of people, mythological gods and goddesses, and mythological scenes.

Shell was an especially popular material for cameos because it was inexpensive, readily obtainable, and easily carved. Shell cameos were worn informally during the day, while those made from rarer and more expensive gems were donned with formal evening wear.

Starting in the eighteenth century, with the dawn of the industrial age, cameos were mass-produced. Historical figures from Russian empress Catherine the Great (1729–1796), to Britain's Queen Victoria (1819–1901), were known to collect cameos.

FOR MORE INFORMATION

Bigelow, Marybelle S. *Fashion in History: Apparel in the Western World.* Minneapolis, MN: Burgess Publishing, 1970.

Miller, Anna M. *Cameos Old and New.* 3rd ed. Woodstock, VT: GemStone Press, 2002.

[See also **Volume 1, Ancient Greece: Cameo and Intaglio**]

Double Watch Fobs

The pocket watch was a valued accessory for men. Breeches had small watch pockets near the front of the waist and watches were attached with fobs, or decorative strings or chains that led from a clip on the waistband to these pockets. From about 1740 until the end of the century, it became very fashionable, especially for well-dressed young men nicknamed *Incroyables,* for the French word for incredible, to display fob ribbons, one on each side of the waist. Occasionally the fob ribbons would hold other decorative ornaments such as seals, or engraved metal disks used for impressing a signature into sealing wax or just for decoration.

FOR MORE INFORMATION

Batterberry, Michael, and Ariane Batterberry. *Fashion: The Mirror of History.* New York: Greenwich House, 1977.

Bigelow, Marybelle S. *Fashion in History: Apparel in the Western World.* Minneapolis, MN: Burgess Publishing, 1970.

Contini, Mila. *Fashion: From Ancient Egypt to the Present Day.* Edited by James Laver. New York: Odyssey Press, 1965.

Cunnington, C. Willett, and Phillis Cunnington. *Handbook of English Costume in the Eighteenth Century.* London, England: Faber and Faber, 1964.

[*See also* **Volume 3, Nineteenth Century: Fobs and Seals**]

Man wearing a jabot, a white linen or cotton neck scarf often trimmed in lace and worn to add decoration to a man's outfit. *Reproduced by permission of the New York Public Library Picture Collection.*

Jabot

A white linen or cotton neck scarf, often trimmed in lace, the jabot worn by men during the eighteenth century added a bit of decoration to a man's outfit. Tied loosely around the neck, the jabot concealed the closure of the shirt, leaving the lace of the jabot to decorate the opening of the waistcoat and the justaucorps, or suit coat. By the end of the century, simpler neck cloths of silk without frills were wrapped around the neck and adorned with a gold stickpin in front. Military men wore black neck cloths while other men wore white ones.

FOR MORE INFORMATION

Bigelow, Marybelle S. *Fashion in History: Apparel in the Western World.* Minneapolis, MN: Burgess Publishing, 1970.

Payne, Blanche, Geitel Winakor, and Jane Farrell-Beck. *The History of Costume.* 2nd ed. New York: HarperCollins, 1992.

■ Nosegay

Sweet smelling flowers, herbs, and perfumes enhanced a person's scent throughout the eighteenth century. The infrequency of bathing made nosegays, or small bouquets, essential for any well-dressed woman. Nosegays could be attached to an outfit or carried. When flowers were pinned or held in small vases at the bustline of a woman's stomacher, the center part of her bodice, they were called bosom flowers or bosom bottles. Real flowers were replaced with rosettes made of perfumed ribbons after about 1750. Nosegays live on into the twenty-first century as the corsages worn for special occasions. ("Corsage" means the bodice of a woman's dress in French. Perhaps nosegays were so often worn attached to the bodice that they came to be called corsages.)

During the eighteenth century, French men began tucking flowers in the

Woman with a nosegay pinned to her dress. The infrequency of bathing had made nosegays, or small floral bouquets, essential for any well-dressed woman in the eighteenth century. *Courtesy of the Library of Congress.*

buttonholes of their waistcoats and introduced boutonières as fashionable nosegays for men. Boutonières were popular among men at formal affairs into the nineteenth century and continue to be worn into the twenty-first century.

FOR MORE INFORMATION

Yarwood, Doreen. *The Encyclopedia of World Costume.* New York: Charles Scribner's Sons, 1978.

Parasols, first invented to protect the user from sun, eventually evolved into a dainty fashion accessory. *Reproduced by permission of © Historical Picture Archive/CORBIS.*

Parasols

Invented to protect people from the sun in ancient Egypt and the Middle East, the parasol was developed as a fashion accessory in late-sixteenth-century Italy and soon spread throughout Europe. A parasol is a light umbrella, generally made of much lighter, less durable materials than an umbrella and not intended to protect the user from rain. At first used only in southern European countries, parasols became popular in England by the mid-eighteenth century and remained an important fashion accessory for women throughout Europe well into the nineteenth century. They were essential to helping women maintain their fashionably pale complexions.

Like other fashionable accessories, the parasol soon became a vehicle for the display of taste and manners. The shades of parasols were made of delicate fabrics like silk, satin, and lace, or of fabrics imprinted with beautiful patterns. Shafts were made of delicately carved wood, and handles might be made of ivory, silver, or gold.

Practicality was soon discarded, and the sizes of parasols grew very tiny, hardly capable of providing shade. In the eighteenth century parasols played an important role in the posturing and posing that became such an important part of social display. Women held a parasol over their shoulder just so, twirled the handle for dramatic effect, and used the parasol to draw attention to themselves.

While it is not surprising that men didn't carry parasols, it also was considered ungentlemanly to carry an umbrella until the nineteenth century. Carrying an umbrella implied that a man couldn't afford a carriage to protect him from the rain, so umbrellas were considered acceptable only for the lower classes. Men using umbrellas in England were mocked as late as the 1780s, but finally people realized that keeping dry might make more sense than keeping in fashion.

FOR MORE INFORMATION

Cassin-Scott, Jack. *Costume and Fashion in Colour, 1550–1760.* Introduction by Ruth M. Green. Dorset, England: Blandford Press, 1975.

Crawford, T. S. *A History of the Umbrella.* Newton Abbot, UK: David and Charles, 1970.

■ Paste Jewelry

Jewelry encrusted with diamonds was worn extensively by the wealthy and coveted by the middle classes throughout the eighteenth century. The expense of real diamonds and other gemstones created a demand for fake jewels. By the end of the seventeenth century lead glass could be faceted and colored to look like cut gemstones and colored foil was placed beneath glass to create the look of sparkling opals. These fake jewels were known as paste. Paste jewelry was much cheaper than real gemstones but also had another advantage: imitation jewels could be made in any size or shape the customer desired. With such freedom, jewelers could create fantastic pieces. During the century intricate floral and bow designs of paste were set in silver and gold. Paste jewelry offered the look of luxury to many more people and became extremely popular by the end of the century, when even the best jewelers made paste jewelry and royalty had copies of real jewelry made in paste. When many people began donating their real jewelry to the cause of the French Revolution (1789–99), the most extravagant designs faded from fashion, but paste jewelry endured as a symbol of affordable beauty.

FOR MORE INFORMATION

Phillips, Clare. *Jewels and Jewelry: 500 Years of Western Jewelry from the World-Renowned Collection of the Victoria and Albert Museum.* New York: Watson-Guptill, 2000.

Reticule

By the last decade of the eighteenth century, women's dresses had changed from heavy, multilayered gowns made of thick fabric to flimsy, lightweight dresses too delicate to hold pockets. At this time reticules, or handbags, became essential for carrying necessities. The first bags were made of lightweight fabric or net and closed with a drawstring. By the nineteenth century reticules had become a source of ridicule, for woman had begun to carry rather full bags, stuffed with all sorts of seemingly frivolous items, including makeup, brushes, and hair ornaments.

FOR MORE INFORMATION

Contini, Mila. *Fashion: From Ancient Egypt to the Present Day.* Edited by James Laver. New York: Odyssey Press, 1965.

Cunnington, C. Willett, and Phillis Cunnington. *Handbook of English Costume in the Eighteenth Century.* London, England: Faber and Faber, 1964.

[*See also* **Volume 3, Nineteenth Century: Pocketbook**]

Sixteenth-century queen Elizabeth I holding a reticule. By the last decade of the eighteenth century, women's dresses were too lightweight and delicate to feature pockets, and reticules, or handbags, came into popularity. *Courtesy of the Library of Congress.*

Snuff Boxes

Europeans first began snorting snuff, the pulverized form of tobacco, in the early seventeenth century, and within one hun-

Snuff boxes came in a variety of sizes and shapes. Often the box was accompanied by a quill or a spoon used to stir the snuff or raise it to the nostrils. *Reproduced by permission of © Massimo Listri/ CORBIS.*

dred years it was widely used by men and women alike. Snuff boxes, tiny decorative containers for the powdered herb, became a symbol of vanity and fashion and an important part of the ritual of using snuff. Snuff was not always taken from a box. Some users preferred to take their snuff from a bottle or a jar, while others carried it loose in their pockets. From the mid-seventeenth century, however, the most common container for snuff was a box, which was an object of much adoration.

Snuff boxes came in a variety of sizes and shapes. Most snuff boxes were three to four inches in diameter, though they became smaller as the use of snuff declined toward the end of the eighteenth century. Often the box was accompanied by a quill or a spoon used to stir the snuff or raise it to the nostrils. Oval was the most common shape for snuff boxes for most of the eighteenth century, with oblong, octagonal, and circular boxes also available. Among the more fanciful shapes were book-shaped boxes, boxes in the form of sedan chairs (portable chairs that can be carried by two attached poles), or those modeled in the form of animals or human figures. The ornament and illustration, including encrusted jewels and enameling, on these beautiful boxes lent them an air of individuality and style that have made them highly prized among collectors to this day.

FOR MORE INFORMATION

Blakemore, Kenneth. *Snuff Boxes.* London, England: F. Muller, 1976.

McCausland, Hugh. *Snuff and Snuff Boxes.* London, England: Batchworth, 1951.

Walking Sticks

First used as a weapon, the walking stick or cane has long been a symbol of strength and power, authority and social prestige, predominantly among men. George Washington (1732–1799), the first American president, carried one, as did later U.S. presidents Ulysses S. Grant (1822–1885) and Warren G. Harding (1865–1923).

The walking stick dates back to ancient times. The Bible makes numerous references to the walking staff as a symbol of office and dignity. Judging from its depiction in paintings, the walking stick became a widely recognized accessory of elegance and social status in the sixteenth and seventeenth centuries. It was during this period that special rules of etiquette developed governing the use of the walking stick, including where and how to carry it.

During the eighteenth century the walking stick gained wider acceptance. Modest canes were used among ordinary people, while those who could afford it opted for walking sticks of great elegance and style. Etiquette rules were greatly relaxed and owners could now safely lean on their canes in casual poses.

The end of the nineteenth century marked a decline in cane styles. While there were still beautiful walking sticks produced during this period, elaborate ornamentation was often used to make up for a lack of form. In the early years of the twentieth century, mass production helped make walking sticks inexpensive and accessible to the masses. The modern crook-handled wooden cane became the standard walking stick for most people.

There were, of course, still attempts to add style to the walking stick. Decorative trim was added to some sticks in the form of silver, gold, or mother-of-pearl inlays. Sometimes the silver handle

First used as a weapon, the walking stick or cane has long been a symbol of strength, power, and social prestige, predominantly among men. *Reproduced by permission of © Hulton-Deutsch Collection/ CORBIS.*

doubled as a pipe holder. The turn-of-the-twentieth-century Oxford stick had a crook handle that held ten cigarettes and a matchbox.

More often than not, however, such flourishes were designed strictly for show, to create a higher commercial grade for the more discriminating purchaser. An affluent walking stick enthusiast might order an ornate cane, but on the whole there was an erosion of style and individuality in the years leading up to World War I (1914–18). The advent of the automobile and modern public transportation rendered the cane less and less useful, necessary only for those whose age or disability required them to use one. Late in the twentieth century, however, recreational goods manufacturers began to sell walking sticks under the name of trekking poles. Made of aluminum and high-tech fibers, with complicated shock absorbing mechanisms, the poles were sold to hikers to help maintain balance at prices over one hundred dollars a pair.

FOR MORE INFORMATION

Hart, Edward. *Walking Sticks.* Marlborough, UK: The Crowood Press, 1986.

Snyder, Jeffrey B. *Canes: From the Seventeenth to the Twentieth Century.* Atglen, PA: Schiffer Publishing, 1997.

[*See also* **Volume 3, Seventeenth Century: Canes**]

Eighteenth-Century Footwear

The display of wealth through fashionable clothes was also seen on the feet in the eighteenth century. Both men and women of wealth wore fancy shoes that signaled their status, a trend that died out by the end of the century.

Women wore high-heeled shoes made of colorful silk or delicate leather, sometimes decorated with gold and silver lace and braid. Although women wore heavily decorated silk dresses, their shoes were rarely made from matching material; to do so would be much too expensive. Some shoes were laced, but most had decorative buckles. The toes of women's shoes were pointed or slightly rounded. These elaborate women's shoes were replaced at the end of the century, however, with much simpler styles, including the especially popular slipper.

For much of the eighteenth century, men's ankles were much admired. Their dark leather shoes with shiny metal buckles highlighted their ankles beneath clinging light colored stockings. The buckles of men's shoes signaled the status of the wearer as well as the importance of the occasion. Buckles could be made simply of steel or brass or encrusted with jewels and engravings. Some men's shoes were colored for special occasions. By mid-century, however, men's ankles were often hidden beneath fashionable jockey boots.

During the eighteenth century shoes and boots were made on straight lasts, or forms that created the soles of shoes, called straights. Without a sole designed specifically for the left or the right foot, shoes were uncomfortable. People frequently switched shoes from one foot to another to reduce the pain. Nevertheless, both men and women were expected to walk smoothly. Children began practicing how to walk properly in shoes from an early age.

FOR MORE INFORMATION

Contini, Mila. *Fashion: From Ancient Egypt to the Present Day.* Edited by James Laver. New York: Odyssey Press, 1965.

Cosgrave, Bronwyn. *The Complete History of Costume and Fashion: From Ancient Egypt to the Present Day.* New York: Checkmark Books, 2000.

Pratt, Lucy, and Linda Woolley. *Shoes.* London, England: V&A Publications, 1999.

The increasing popularity of horseracing triggered a fashion for jockey boots in the mid-eighteenth century, and young men began wearing them for everyday wear. *Reproduced by permission of Getty Images.*

Jockey Boots

At the beginning of the century, low shoes were the most fashionable footwear for men. Showing a man's ankles was especially fashionable. Boots were only worn by military officers or by others for traveling, riding a horse, or hunting. The increasing popularity of horseracing triggered a fashion for jockey boots in the mid-eighteenth century, and young men began wearing jockey boots for everyday wear. Jockey boots were tall, dark leather boots with a rounded toe. The boot top had loops designed for making it easier to pull the boots on and tops that folded over to show a contrasting color of leather lining the boot. Jockey boots were worn by a select few, but the fashion for wearing them ushered in the larger trend for boots in the nineteenth century.

FOR MORE INFORMATION

Cosgrave, Bronwyn. *The Complete History of Costume and Fashion: From Ancient Egypt to the Present Day.* New York: Checkmark Books, 2000.

Pratt, Lucy, and Linda Woolley. *Shoes.* London, England: V&A Publications, 1999.

[*See also* **Volume 3, Nineteenth Century: Boots**]

Slippers

After the French Revolution (1789–99), people began to reject obvious signs of wealth. The large buckles and elaborate patterned silk shoes of earlier days were replaced with simple, plain flat-soled slippers. Slippers were made of thin kid, the skin of a baby goat, or cloth. The toes of slippers were either pointed or rounded, and the throat of the shoe, or the opening at the top of the foot, was cut into a U or V shape. The throat was left plain or a small bow was added. Slippers were often dyed to match a woman's pelisse (a light-weight coat), sash, or gloves. Light colors of green, pink, and purple were popular. Slippers first became popular for women, but by the nineteenth century men wore black slippers to formal events as well.

FOR MORE INFORMATION

Cosgrave, Bronwyn. *The Complete History of Costume and Fashion: From Ancient Egypt to the Present Day.* New York: Checkmark Books, 2000.

Pratt, Lucy, and Linda Woolley. *Shoes.* London, England: V&A Publications, 1999.

Nineteenth-Century Industrialization

The nineteenth century witnessed an amazing transformation in the political and economic life of Europeans and Americans alike. During the first decade of the century almost all of Europe was under the power of France's ruler, Napoleon Bonaparte (1769–1821), or other members of his family who controlled the outer regions of the empire. With widespread support for overturning the old systems of Europe, Napoleon had built a vast French empire. Although Napoleon was defeated in 1814 at Waterloo and the French, Austrian, and Prussian monarchies' power was restored, it did not take long for revolution to unsettle the royals' power once again. Throughout Europe and the United States, the new technologies of the Industrial Revolution transformed economies based on large farms to those based on industrial production, which created a wealthy middle class. Possessing economic power, these merchants and industrialists also wanted political power, which the monarchical systems of government denied them. By the end of the nineteenth century many of the older European empires had split into the independent states of Italy, Germany, France, and Russia, carving the way for the growth of the modern-day nations.

As the political boundaries and rulers of countries changed during the century, the economies of Europe and America grew rapidly. By the end of the eighteenth century, Great Britain had

INVENTIONS THAT CHANGED THE WORLD OF FASHION

The Industrial Revolution of the eighteenth and nineteenth centuries had a direct effect on how clothing materials were made. Four innovations in particular helped change fashion: the cotton gin, spinning jenny, sewing machine, and artificial dye.

Cotton Gin

For most of the eighteenth century, cotton was an exotic commodity because it was difficult to process—it took one slave ten hours to separate one pound of cotton lint from its seeds. In 1793, a Yale University graduate named Eli Whitney (1765–1825) visited a plantation in Savannah, Georgia, and designed a machine to remove cotton seeds from lint. His cotton gin worked by placing cotton into a hopper, where the cotton would be held back while a rotating drum with wires would pull the cotton away. As a result of Whitney's invention, cotton became the American South's leading cash crop, supplying Great Britain with most of its cotton. Where the South had once produced little more than sixty tons of cotton a year, by 1840 the South was generating a million tons of cotton a year. Indirectly, the cotton gin meant that more slaves would be needed to pick cotton. Within thirty years of Whitney's invention, the number of American slaves had tripled.

Spinning Jenny

The spinning jenny was an eighteenth century modification of the familiar spinning wheel. One day in the 1750s, English carpenter James Hargreaves (1720–1778) inadvertently knocked over his spinning wheel in his Lancashire, England, home and was startled to see it, on its side, still spinning. He instantly envisioned a series of spinning wheels similarly aligned; such a device, he realized, could approximate the rhythm of human fingers. Following a decade of fits and starts Hargreaves completed his spinning jenny in 1768. The population of existing spinners saw Hargreaves's invention as a threat to their livelihood, because one jenny could do the work of several men. The spinners turned violent. A group of them formed a vigilante mob, stormed into Hargreaves's home, and destroyed his inventions. He moved his family to neighboring Nottingham, and opened a mill where he manufactured yarn until his death. However,

grown into the dominant economic power in Europe, surpassing France and Spain. The trade routes established between Europe and the rest of the world during the eighteenth century promoted the production of manufactured goods and laid the foundation for the expansion of industrialization in Great Britain and, eventually, in other countries. During the first seventy years of the nineteenth century Great Britain developed the first industrial society, with unprecedented trade, urban, and population growth. The factory systems developed in Great Britain soon spread to the rest of Europe—especially Belgium, France, and Germany—and America. Industrialization brought rapid growth of cities and factories, and with them the expansion of the middle- and working-class populations. The expanding middle classes put pressure on their govern-

he was unsuccessful in obtaining a patent for his invention.

Sewing Machines

The most significant fashion-related invention of the 1800s, the sewing machine, was the work of several men. French tailor Barthelemy Thimmonier (1793–1859) invented a machine in 1830 which used a hooked needle to make chain stitches. Threatened by the efficiency of Thimmonier's machine, local tailors formed a mob and attacked Thimmonier and destroyed his invention. In 1846, American inventor Elias Howe (1819–1867) patented a sewing machine which made lock stitches with an eye-pointed needle. Howe's invention did not sell well, but with the addition of Isaac Singer (1811–1875) and Allen Wilson's (1824–1888) modifications, which made Howe's invention work more easily and efficiently, the sewing machine became quite popular when the first home sewing machine was sold in 1889.

Artificial Dyes

From biblical times through the mid-nineteenth century, people derived dyes from solely natural resources, such as the indigo or sumac plant or the shellfish. The first synthetic, or man-made, dye was only created in 1856, when an eighteen-year-old British chemist named William Henry Perkin (1838–1907) was attempting to synthesize quinine when he mixed aniline together with a solution of alcohol and potassium dichromate. The unexpected result was mauveine, a purple dye that became very popular in Great Britain. Queen Victoria (1819–1901) wore mauve to her daughter's wedding, and even British postage stamps were dyed with mauveine. Perkin's mentor, German scientist August Wilhelm von Hofmann (1818–1892), was inspired by his student's discovery to develop his own dyes, and within a few years Hofmann created rosaniline, a reddish-brown dye made from aniline and carbon tertrachloride. Within only a few years, in 1868, German chemist Carl Graebe (1841–1927) created alizarin, a synthetic vegetable dye.

Each of these inventions, in their own way, made clothing faster, easier, and cheaper to make. The result continues to be felt in the ever changing fashions marketed each new season throughout the world.

ments to gain political influence throughout the Western world. Soon wealthy landowners were joined by wealthy merchants and factory owners in government, and life was forever changed for working people. In general, people became richer and could afford more luxuries than ever before.

The introduction of life's luxuries

Industrialization, or the manufacture or production of goods on a large scale, offered the luxuries of life to more people than ever before. The Industrial Revolution had brought the construction of canals and railways across Europe and America. These canals and railways created national and even broader markets by transporting goods manufactured in new factories great distances. Besides transporting goods to more corners of Western civilization than ever before, railways also transported people. Travel had once been available to only the wealthiest people. The rise of industry throughout the Western world increased production and the increased wealth of the majority of people encouraged many to travel more widely and purchase more goods than ever before. The leisure of travel opened doors to new ways of life for many. Leisure activities also required new outfits and soon people were wearing special bathing costumes and tennis outfits.

As the century continued, more inventions increased the ease with which people lived and communicated with each other. Cheap postal services were introduced and magazines began to circulate nationally and internationally. The telegraph could electronically transmit information instantly from one end of a country to another. The International Exhibition of 1851 held in London displayed thousands of these inventions from around the world, including a new product called rubber, a locomotive that could travel at sixty miles-per-hour, cameras, printing presses, and a variety of intricately woven fabrics. During the 140 days it was open, nearly six million people traveled to see the exhibition and sample the new inventions. By the end of the nineteenth century, the Europeans and Americans had fully embraced the benefits of industrialization. By the end of the nineteenth century, the first advertising, chains of retail stores, and widely-circulating magazines combined with the efficient manufacturing systems and trade routes to transform the Western world into a mass consumer society. The rise of consumer spending would bring clothes of reasonable quality, as well as the shifting trends of fashion, to more people than ever before.

FOR MORE INFORMATION

Bridgman, Roger Francis. *1000 Inventions and Discoveries.* New York: DK Publishing, 2002.

Carlson, Laurie. *Queen of Inventions: How the Sewing Machine Changed the World.* North Clinton, UT: Milbrook Press, 2003.

Collins, Mary. *The Industrial Revolution.* Danbury, CT: Children's Press, 2000.

Costume Illustration: The Nineteenth Century. Introduction by James Laver. London, England: Victoria and Albert Museum, 1947.

Fletcher, Marion. *Female Costume in the Nineteenth Century.* (National Gallery Booklets) Melbourne: Oxford University Press, 1966.

Garfield, Simon. *Mauve: How One Man Invented a Color That Changed the World.* New York: W. W. Norton, 2001.

Gibbs-Smith, Charles H. *The Fashionable Lady in the 19th Century.* London, England: Her Majesty's Stationery Office, 1960.

Kellogg Ann T., et al. *In an Influential Fashion: An Encyclopedia of Nineteenth- and Twentieth-Century Fashion Designers and Retailers Who Transformed Dress.* Westport, CT: Greenwood Press, 2002.

Poggio, Pier Paolo, and Carlo Simoni. *The Industrial Revolution, 1800–1850.* Broomall, PA: Chelsea House Publishers, 2003.

Nineteenth-Century Clothing

Dress during the nineteenth century changed dramatically. The change was influenced by shifts in taste, of course, but more significantly by the introduction of machines to the construction of clothing. Sewing machines, power looms, or weaving machines, steam power, electricity, new dye formulas, and other inventions increased the speed and ease of clothing manufacture. These inventions were used to add embellishments to women's clothing; machine-made trimmings were applied in bulk to the enormous

Nineteenth-century industrialization offered the luxuries of life to more people than ever before. Sewing machines, electricity, new dye formulas, and other inventions increased the speed and ease of clothing manufacture. *Reproduced by permission of © Historical Picture Archive/CORBIS.*

CHARLES FREDERICK WORTH INDUSTRIALIZES FASHION

Though born and raised in England, Charles Frederick Worth (1825–1895) became the first world famous French fashion designer. He was also the first to create and employ the principles of design and fashion that would be called "haute couture," or "high fashion." Worth not only designed clothes for much of Europe's nobility and many American millionaires, he also introduced many modern changes in the ways clothing was designed, made, and sold.

Worth was born in 1825 in Lincolnshire, in the east of England. His father was a lawyer who had lost most of his money gambling, so young Charles was forced to go out to work when he was only eleven. He worked for many years at a department store, then at a company that sold fabrics. Through his sales experience he learned about what women wanted and needed in clothing and fashion. He wished to become a dress designer, so at the age of twenty he took a job with a fabric firm in Paris, where he could study design while he worked. It was there that he introduced his first new idea of offering dress design to customers at the fabric company. For the first time, ladies could get the whole dress, design and fabric, at the same location.

Before Worth began his design career, dresses had been made by dressmakers, and designs had been created by the customer and the dressmaker, who got ideas from looking at pictures of popular dresses. Worth was one of the first designers to come up with his own ideas, based on his knowledge of women's needs. Soon he started his own company. The wife of the Austrian ambassador bought a dress from Worth that attracted the notice of the Empress of France. Worth became the court designer, and was soon making dresses for the royalty of

Russia, Italy, Spain, and Austria. Famous and wealthy Americans such as the Vanderbilts and the Astors also came to the House of Worth for special gowns, making Worth the first celebrity fashion designer.

Worth used beautiful and luxurious fabrics for his dresses, and he trimmed them with rich decoration, such as fringe, lace, braid, and tassels made of pearls. His many important contributions to design included an ankle-length walking skirt, shockingly short for its time, and the princess gown, a waist-less dress that hung simple and straight in the front while draping in full pleats in the back.

However, more lasting have been Worth's contributions to fashion as an industry. He changed the way dresses were shown to customers by being the first designer to use living women as models, and the first to have fashion shows to reveal his new designs to customers. He also began to make high fashion more widely available, by selling his designs not only to individual customers but also to other dressmakers, clothing manufacturers, and to the newly invented department stores. Another introduction Worth made was the practice of mass-producing parts of a piece of clothing, then putting them together in different ways. For example, a certain type of sleeve could be produced in a bulk quantity, and then used on several different types of dresses to produce a different look each time.

Worth's ideas came at a time when clothing factories and department stores were new developments, and they combined well to create a new concept in fashion called ready-to-wear clothing. For the first time, people could simply go to a store and buy the latest fashions, and "haute couture" style was no longer only available to the rich. Charles Worth died in 1895, but his sons continued to operate his successful design house for many years.

flowing gowns worn by women in midcentury. By the end of the century, the introduction of ditto suits for men increased men's interest in ready-to-wear clothing, which would ruin many tailors' careers by the mid-twentieth century since the clothes did not need alterations.

The style of dress worn by men became increasingly somber and less flamboyant throughout the century. At the beginning of the century, stylishly dressed men known as dandies, such as George "Beau" Brummell, influenced male fashions by replacing fancy outfits of ornate waistcoats and ruffles with plain dark jackets, high-collared shirts and simple cravats, vests, and eventually trousers. Although some men wore corsets and loud clothing during the century, by the end of the period proper male clothing came to be associated more with clean, polished clothing rather than with fancy ornament. The color black, introduced during this century as proper for male dress attire, has endured to the present day in the form of tuxedos and dark suits.

Women's fashions shifted dramatically throughout the century. Starting with styles that revealed more of the female figure than ever before in Europe and America, women shifted to wearing large dresses with huge sleeves and skirts and heavy ornamentation by midcentury. As the century continued, women's fashions changed again to incorporate slimmer silhouettes, or profiles, with the fullness of the skirt limited to the rear bustle. Despite the huge variations in skirt and sleeve size, women's waists were pinched tighter and tighter in a variety of constrictive corsets throughout the century. The importance of a slim waist throughout the nineteenth century influenced some mothers to confine their young daughters in binding corsets as well.

While the styles for men at the end of the century laid the foundation that would influence men's clothing for the centuries to come, the styles for women did not. Women's fashion began to be influenced by fashion designers, the first being Charles Frederick Worth (1825–1895). And in the coming century, women would experience much more liberty and a variety of new styles would emerge to reflect this. One style introduced during the nineteenth century would have a lasting impact on the fashion of both men and women across the globe: Starting as a sturdy work pant, blue jeans would become one of the most influential American fashion trends.

FOR MORE INFORMATION

Byrde, Penelope. *Nineteenth Century Fashion*. London, England: B. T. Batsford, 1992.

Cosgrave, Bronwyn. *The Complete History of Costume and Fashion: From Ancient Egypt to the Present Day*. New York: Checkmark Books, 2000.

Costume Illustration: The Nineteenth Century. Introduction by James Laver. London, England: Victoria and Albert Museum, 1947.

DeMarly, Diana. *Worth: Father of Haute Couture*. New York: Holmes and Meier, 1990.

Fletcher, Marion. *Female Costume in the Nineteenth Century*. (National Gallery Booklets) Melbourne: Oxford University Press, 1966.

Gibbs-Smith, Charles H. *The Fashionable Lady in the 19th Century*. London, England: Her Majesty's Stationery Office, 1960.

Moers, Ellen. *The Dandy: Brummell to Beerbohm*. New York: Viking Press, 1960.

Payne, Blanche, Geitel Winakor, and Jane Farrell-Beck. *The History of Costume*. 2nd ed. New York: HarperCollins, 1992.

Yarwood, Doreen. *Fashion in the Western World: 1500–1900*. New York: Drama Book Publishers, 1992.

Bathing Costumes

The development of special clothing for swimming went through important changes during the 1800s and early 1900s. Though people of various cultures had bathed in oceans, rivers, and lakes for centuries, the nineteenth century saw a dramatic rise in the popularity of swimming as a recreational activity. Late in the eighteenth century, scientists had learned more about the causes of disease which in turn rid the Western world of a fear of bathing, and people began to embrace the water as a delightful recreation and sport. Railroads, newly built across Europe and the United States, enabled people to travel more easily, and many took the new trains to seaside resorts where they could relax on the beach and swim in the ocean. These vacationers began to demand less burdensome clothing for their beach activities.

The extreme modesty of the Victorian period (relating to the conservative times of Britain's Queen Victoria [1837–1901]) required that bathing costumes cover almost as much of the body as regular street clothes. During the first half of the century, women wore heavy bathing dresses made of wool, with corsets underneath. These bulky dresses were quite heavy once they were wet, and some ladies increased the weight further by sewing weights into the hems of their skirts to prevent them from floating up in the water. Women wearing these early Victorian costumes did little actual swimming and instead bobbed or splashed in the water. Active swimming was seen as an activity for men.

Men were allowed a bit more freedom in bathing dress, though they still remained modestly covered in long sleeveless woolen jerseys over knee-length trousers. It was illegal in most places for men to expose their chests, and many beaches required men to have a modesty skirt, a piece of loose fabric covering their genital area.

During the 1860s, as women began to gain more social freedom, sportswear was introduced for the more active woman. Among the new sports outfits was a daring modern bathing costume. Similar to the clothing men wore to swim, the new bathing suits had three parts: a short belted dress, knee-length bloomers, and dark stockings. Though the new suits offered more freedom of movement, they were still made of heavy wool. As the century progressed, the sleeves became shorter, until, by the early 1900s, women too wore sleeveless bathing dresses. Less weighted down by their clothes, women began to join men in active swimming and in demanding still more practical and revealing swimwear. In 1907, famous Australian swimmer Annette Kellerman (1887–1975) was arrested for appearing on a New Jersey beach in a knee-length sleeveless one-piece bathing suit. However, by the 1920s, the one-piece suit had become common beachwear for both men and women.

As women began to gain more social freedom during the late 1800s, sportswear, including a daring new bathing costume, was introduced for the more active woman. *Reproduced by permission of © CORBIS.*

FOR MORE INFORMATION

Lenacek, Lena. *Making Waves: Swimsuits and the Undressing of America.* San Francisco, CA: Chronicle Books, 1989.

Martin, Richard. *Splash!: A History of Swimwear.* New York: Rizzoli, 1990.

[*See also* **Volume 4, 1919–29: Swimwear**]

The Betsy

A ruffled collar of gathered lace, the betsy, also spelled betsey and betsie, of the early 1800s was an updated variation on the starched linen ruff that had been popular during the sixteenth century. When the ruff reappeared in early nineteenth century England, it was smaller and simpler, a strip of lace gathered and tied around the neck with a drawstring. Its unmistakable resemblance to the tall ruff worn by Queen Elizabeth (1533–1603) gave the betsy its name, after Beth or Bets, nicknames for Elizabeth. However, while the ruff of the 1500s had been made of linen or lace and held in stiff pleats with starch, the later version was made of lacy fabric like tulle, a sheer silk or cotton, and was simply pulled into soft gathers.

The nineteenth century opened with a preference for simple styles in women's clothing. Inspired by the fascination with Greek styles that had followed the French Revolution (1789–99), several different styles of simple tunic dresses became popular throughout Europe. These dresses were high-necked, high-waisted and loose, with uncomplicated flowing lines. The gathered betsy was a popular accessory to the plain turn-of-the-century gown. Soft and feminine, the betsy decorated the high neckline and gave the wearer the look of one of the heroines of the romantic novels which were becoming popular at the time.

FOR MORE INFORMATION

Bigelow, Marybelle S. *Fashion in History: Apparel in the Western World.* Minneapolis, MN: Burgess Publishing, 1970.

Yarwood, Doreen. *Fashion in the Western World: 1500–1900.* New York: Drama Book Publishers, 1992.

[*See also* **Volume 3, Sixteenth Century: Ruffs**]

Bloomers

Long, loose pants that are gathered at the ankle, bloomers were worn by women during the nineteenth century both as outerwear and as underwear. Bloomers were part of a movement toward more practical clothing for women, and soon became closely identified with suffragists (women working for women's right to vote) and feminists (women working to improve the status of women). Many men were angry with the suffragists, and did not like women wearing pants, so they often ridiculed the new bloomer outfits.

As early as the 1820s some women had designed and worn a practical garment for traveling and other activities. This garment consisted of a knee-length dress over a loose pair of trousers gathered at the waist and ankle. The "bloomer dress" as it would come to be called, covered the wearer completely so that it provided the modesty that the times required. At the same time, it provided much more freedom of movement than the tight corsets and trailing skirts that most women wore.

In the mid-1800s, feminist writer and editor Amelia Bloomer (1818–1894) wrote favorably about the new outfit in her newspaper *The Lily,*

Long, loose pants that are gathered at the ankle, bloomers were worn by women during the nineteenth century both as outerwear and as underwear. *Reproduced by permission of Simon & Schuster.*

and soon the new pants were dubbed "bloomers." Many men and women laughed at the new fashion, but some women found it very comfortable and sensible for such activities as bicycling, playing tennis, and travelling. In the United States, many women who traveled to the undeveloped West in wagon trains wore bloomers.

Though bloomers were not widely accepted as outerwear in the nineteenth century, they did become popular underpants for women and girls, and by the late 1800s, most women wore long, loose cotton bloomers under their long skirts instead of petticoats.

FOR MORE INFORMATION

Bloomer, Amelia. "True History of the So-Called Bloomer Costume." *Religio-Philosophical Journal.* December 28, 1889. On *Ephemera.* http://www.spirithistory.com/blomer.html (accessed on August 6, 2003).

Gattey, Charles Nelson. *The Bloomer Girls.* New York: Coward-McCann, 1967.

■ Blue Jeans

Durable, heavy-duty pants made from dark blue cotton fabric, blue jeans were first created as work pants for the gold miners of the 1849 California gold rush, a time when people of the United States rapidly moved into California in search of gold. Once worn only by those who did heavy manual labor, jeans became one of the most popular and common clothing items of the twentieth century. Blue jeans moved from work clothes to the preferred pants of rebellious young men during the 1950s and 1960s to high fashion items. By the end of the twentieth century, a comfortable pair of jeans had become a necessity in the casual wardrobe of both men and women. Though they are bought, sold, and worn in almost every country in the world, blue jeans are still regarded as a fundamentally American garment.

The word "jeans" had been used since the 1600s to describe the rough clothing worn by working men, because this type of clothing was often made of sturdy jean, or *genes* fabric from Genoa, Italy. Denim, the durable fabric which is almost always used to make modern blue jeans, was originally made in Nîmes, France. American manufacturers shortened the name *serge de Nîmes,* to denim. Denim fabric was often dyed dark blue so that work clothes made from it would not show dirt and stains.

The first blue jeans were created by teamwork between a tailor, Jacob Davis, and a merchant, Levi Strauss, who were both interested in making a profit by selling clothing to the thousands of miners drawn to the California gold rush. Strauss was selling tent fabric, work clothes, and other supplies to miners when he was approached in 1873 by Davis, a tailor who had developed the idea of making work clothes stronger by putting copper rivets, or fasteners, at certain points, like pockets, which were likely to tear. Together, Davis and Strauss began to make what they called "waist overalls" out of sturdy denim fabric with copper rivets. Over the years, the pants came to be called jeans or Levis.

Over the next decades, the popularity of blue jeans spread among working people, such as farmers and the ranchers of the American West. Jeans became so popular among cowboys that during the 1930s, a company called Wrangler formed just to make denim work clothing for those who rode the range. In the 1920s, 1930s, and 1940s many people began spending their spare time at the movies, where popular Western films found glamour and romance in the adventures of the cowboys who rode horses, shot bad guys, and wore blue jeans. Those who wished to imitate the casual, rugged look of the cowboys they saw in films began to wear jeans as casual wear.

During World War II (1939–45) blue jeans became part of the official uniform of the Navy and Coast Guard, and became even more popular when worn as off-duty leisure clothing by many other soldiers. During the 1950s many young people began to wear jeans when they saw them on rebellious young American film stars such as Marlon Brando (1924–) and James Dean (1931–1955). Blue jeans were so identified with American culture that they were placed in the American exhibit at the 1958 World's Fair. Around the same time, the first jeans were exported to Europe.

The rebellious image of blue jeans continued into the 1960s and 1970s, when the nonconformist hippie youth made ragged, patched blue jeans part of their uniform. Jeans had become extremely popular, but were still mainly worn by working people or the young.

AMERICAN COWBOY

The American cowboy roamed the plains west of the Mississippi River in the mid- to late nineteenth century. His job involved tending cattle, usually miles from where he lived and for months at a time. The cowboy developed a functional manner of dress that suited his unique lifestyle. Some of the key elements of cowboy attire have entered into the American popular imagination and become symbols of a romantic and lost way of life.

The American cowboys borrowed much of their clothing, along with many of their customs, from the earlier *vaqueros,* herdsmen of Mexican and American Indian descent who migrated northward over the Rio Grande River into Texas. Necessity also dictated a lot of the cowboy's attire. A cowboy had to carry everything he might need with him on his horse. He was plagued by many dangers, including hostile American Indians, rattlesnakes, cattle rustlers, sudden rainstorms, flooding rivers, and stampeding cattle. Virtually everything the cowboy wore or kept close at hand was designed to help him overcome these obstacles.

A typical cowboy outfit consisted of a muslin (sheer cotton fabric) shirt with a waistcoat, similar to a vest, and denim or buckskin trousers. To protect his legs when riding through thorny brush, the cowboy wore a set of leggings called chaps, an abbreviation of chaparejos, the Spanish word for the leggings, over his trousers. Chaps were made of leather or animal hide, often with the fur left on the outside, and covered only the front of the legs to allow for freedom of movement. Fur chaps made of bear and goat were used on the northern ranges. Chaps were attached by a belt at the waist and ties along the back of the legs. Some early chaps were fringed at the seams.

Another essential component of cowboy style was the wide-brimmed hat, designed to protect the wearer from the harsh elements of the open plain, especially the blistering sun. Cowboy hats added an element of individuality to the cowboy's attire. Often the cowboy would make his own hat. There were regional distinctions as well. It was said that you could tell where a cowboy came from by the shape of his hat. The most famous cowboy hat of all was designed by John B. Stetson of Philadelphia, Pennsylvania. Stetson hats were made of wool felt with a large brim and oval, cylindrical crown. So many cowboys wore Stetson hats that the hats came to be known as "Boss of the Plains" and became a symbol of the American West.

A kerchief tied loosely around the neck performed a variety of functions for the cowboy. He could use it to protect his mouth and nose from dust, cover the back of his neck to prevent sunburn, or

During the 1980s this began to change as famous fashion designers created designer jeans, which were expensive and became fashionable wear for many occasions. By the end of the twentieth century, blue jeans had become one of the most widely worn items of clothing in the world. In 2001 a pair of Levis dating from the 1880s and found buried under layers of mud in Nevada was sold at auction for over forty-five thousand dollars.

FOR MORE INFORMATION

Harris, Alice. *The Blue Jean.* New York: PowerHouse Books, 2002.

tie it around his head to keep his hat from blowing off on windy days. It could even be used as a makeshift sling for a broken arm. Red was the preferred color for these versatile bandannas, often called wipes.

Still popular in the twenty-first century is the cowboy boot. It was the most expensive part of the cowboy's wardrobe. Store-bought boots sold for seven dollars in 1880, while tailor-made models could go for as much as fifteen dollars. A high "Cuban heel" prevented the wearer's foot from slipping through his stirrup. When dismounting from a horse, the heels dug into the ground to ensure good footing. Early cowboy boots had square toes, though round and pointed styles eventually came into fashion. By the 1890s fancy cowboy boots were being sold through mail-order catalogs.

Cowboys first captured the public imagination during the large-scale cattle drives north from Texas in the period just after the American Civil War (1861–65). Their numbers steadily decreased with the decline of the open range and the advent of homesteading, the establishment of houses and farms on open land. While the cowboy era lasted barely a generation, the cowboy style lived on in the form of dime novels, movie serials, and television programs and remains a popular style of dress for many people in the United States.

A typical cowboy outfit consisted of a kerchief around the neck and denim or buckskin trousers. To protect his legs the cowboy wore a set of leggings called "chaps," and the wide-brimmed hat protected his head. *Courtesy of the Library of Congress.*

Lindmier, Tom, and Steve Mount. *I See by Your Outfit: Historic Cowboy Gear of the Northern Plains.* Glendo, WY: High Plains Press, 1996.

Reedstrom, E. Lisle. *Authentic Costumes and Characters of the Old West.* New York: Sterling Publishers, 1992.

Weidt, Maryanne N. *Mr. Blue Jeans: A Story about Levi Strauss.* Minneapolis, MN: Carolrhoda Books, 1990.

[*See also* **Volume 5, 1980–2003: Designer Jeans**]

Coats

Following the American and French Revolutions of the late 1700s, an appreciation for democracy and for the common man spread over the Western world. This led to a plainer style of dress for the men of the 1800s than had been the fashion in the centuries before. Elaborate frills and fancy decorations were replaced by simple styles in basic colors. The coat was one of the central elements of the nineteenth-century man's everyday wardrobe, and, though there were many different popular styles, they all reflected the less showy fashion of the times.

During the early 1800s, the desired masculine shape featured a large chest and a small waist, and the coats of the day were designed to help achieve this figure. Shoulders and chests were often padded to make the top appear larger, and coattails were cut full to emphasize the slim waist. Depending on the wealth of the wearer coats were made of wool, cotton, or linen, and different fabrics were worn in different weather. The most popular coat styles of the first part of the century were the frock coat and the cutaway coat. Both were rather formal coats with a design based on the British hunting coat, cut up to the waist in the front with long tails in the back. The cutaway had a curved line along the side and rounded tails in the back, while the frock coat was cut in a straight line to a pair of pointed coat tails in the back. Frock coats also had a trim piece at the back waist with two buttons for decoration. The frock coat remained the most common coat for daytime wear into the 1890s. However, while bright reds, greens, and yellows were popular in the early 1800s, by the second half of the century most men wore only dark colored coats, such as black and navy.

The fitted silhouette of the coats of the early 1800s was replaced at midcentury by straight-cut jackets that hung loose from shoulder to hip. Another development during the second half of the century was the introduction of special clothing for sports. In 1837 the captain of the British ship H.M.S. *Blazer* outfitted his men in a short boxy double-breasted (two rows of buttons down the front) jacket. The new style caught on and "blazers" became popular wear for such sporting activities as boating and tennis. In 1890 the

Norfolk jacket was introduced; it was a hip-length loose coat which was meant to be worn with the knee pants called knickerbockers. The Norfolk and knickers, or knee-length pants, soon became popular casual wear for men and boys of all classes.

Men of the 1800s also had a variety of overcoats to choose from. For those who preferred an old-fashioned look, cloaks were still acceptable, such as the dramatic Garrick, which was a long velvet cape trimmed with fur. The Chesterfield was the most common modern coat, a long, straight-cut single-breasted coat, usually made of black wool with a velvet collar. Some stylish men wore buffalo or beaver fur coats that reached their ankles, while others preferred the dashing look of the Inverness, a sleeveless wool plaid coat with a short cape that hung from the collar around the shoulders.

FOR MORE INFORMATION

Bigelow, Marybelle S. *Fashion in History: Western Dress, Prehistoric to Present*. Minneapolis, MN: Burgess Publishing, 1970.

Laver, James. *Costume and Fashion: A Concise History*. New York: Thames and Hudson, 2002.

Crinoline

Full crinoline underskirts were necessities of popular women's fashions of the mid-1800s. As skirt styles became fuller during the century, women were burdened by having to wear several layers of petticoats, or stiff, heavy, and uncomfortable, fabric underskirts. Petticoats were replaced by lightweight hoop crinolines, which allowed skirt styles to expand even further.

The word crinoline comes from the French word *crin,* meaning "horsehair," because early crinolines were made from horsehair and wool. Elegant ladies of the mid-nineteenth century wore very wide skirts, and stiff horsehair crinolines held the skirts out from the body. Some crinolines measured more than four yards around the bottom, and women wearing these skirts had to move carefully to avoid knocking things off of tables as they moved around a room.

The hoop crinoline was made of a series of steel rings, which got gradually bigger in size, connected by cotton tape into a sort of cage that fit under a skirt to hold it out. *Reproduced by permission of © Bettmann/ CORBIS.*

It was said that an average-sized room could hold only two or three women wearing crinolines.

Around 1850, women were much relieved when a new kind of crinoline was invented. The hoop crinoline, as it was called, was made of a series of steel rings, which got gradually bigger in size, connected by cotton tape into a sort of cage that fit under a skirt to hold it out. Though the new hoops were much lighter weight and more comfortable than the old horsehair crinolines, they still had one similar problem: if a woman was not very careful when she sat down, her skirt would swing up in front of her, exposing her underpants. This was a serious problem in a time of great modesty, when the sight of a woman's ankle was considered shocking. The wide skirts also made it impossible for women to sit down in carriages, and a woman travelling often had to kneel or sit on the carriage floor.

By the late 1880s, women had had enough of the inconveniences of extremely wide skirts and crinolines passed out of fashion as slimmer, more tailored-looking skirts became popular.

FOR MORE INFORMATION

Batterberry, Michael, and Ariane Batterberry. *Fashion: The Mirror of History.* New York: Greenwich House, 1982.

Bigelow, Marybelle S. *Fashion in History: Apparel in the Western World.* Minneapolis, MN: Burgess Publishing, 1970.

[*See also* **Volume 3, Sixteenth Century: Farthingales; Volume 3, Seventeenth Century: Petticoats**]

Dinner Jacket

The dinner jacket emerged from an era when it was considered proper for upper-class men to dress formally for the evening meal. A comfortable, less formal alternative to a tailcoat, a jacket with long flaps in the back, the dinner jacket, or tuxedo jacket as it is sometimes called, has become the most common type of men's formal wear since the 1890s.

While upper-class formal wear for Western men had been frilly during the 1700s, the 1800s saw the introduction of a more restrained, tailored style. The particularly fashionable British writer Edward Bulwer-Lytton (1803–1873) popularized the color black both for men's formal and everyday wear, and by the mid-1800s men's formal dress was largely defined as "white tie and tails," that is, a white bow tie worn with a stiff white shirt front and a black coat with long tails in the back.

By the late 1800s clothing styles were beginning to become slightly looser. While vacationing at his estate in Cowes, England, the British prince of Wales, Edward VII (1841–1910), sought a more comfortable alternative to the usual formal dinner attire. His tailor modified a popular military-style short black jacket called a mess jacket, to cre-

The dinner jacket emerged from an era when it was considered proper for upper-class men to dress formally for the evening meal. *Reproduced by permission of © Bettmann/CORBIS.*

ate a semiformal dinner jacket for the prince. The new jacket was dubbed the "Cowes jacket," after the first place it was worn.

In 1886 the prince had an American named James Potter as a guest at his country estate. Potter liked Prince Edward's new formal wear and had a jacket made for himself. When he wore his new dinner jacket at the elite upper-class resort of Tuxedo Park in New York, it instantly became popular. Alternatively, some historians report that a New York socialite named Griswold Lorillard cut the tails off his formal coat in 1886 at the Tuxedo Park Autumn Ball, starting the fad. In either case, the new jacket soon took on the name of the resort and became known simply as a tuxedo.

In 1930 Philadelphia tailors Marliss and Max Rudolphker produced the first mass-marketed ready-to-wear tuxedos. During the economically depressed 1930s, dashing tuxedos became a symbol of hope, as Hollywood movies popularized not only the black "tux" but also the white dinner jacket and the velvet and brocade versions called smoking jackets.

Dinner jackets have remained the fundamental ingredient of men's formal attire into the 2000s. Though each decade has seen slight alterations, wide lapels during the 1920s, narrow lapels during the 1930s, bright-colored brocades during the 1960s and 1970s, the basic style has changed little from Edward VII's original Cowes jacket. While "white tie" formal occasions still call for a tailcoat, far more common is the "black tie" occasion, which demands that men wear a tuxedo.

FOR MORE INFORMATION

Belkin, Lisa. "A Party for the Tuxedo at 100: Suit Regains Its Popularity." *The New York Times* (May 10, 1986): 17, 35.

Boyer, G. B., and Henry Wolf. "R.S.V.P. Black Tie." *Town & Country* (June 1986): 124–31.

Ditto Suits

The mid-nineteenth century saw the introduction of a type of men's suit that would become the dominant form of Western men's dress clothing of the next century. The ditto suit, as it was called, featured a jacket, vest, and trousers made from the same fabric. Also called the sack suit, the new style was characterized by a loose-fitting jacket which hung straight from the shoulders with no seam or fitting at the waist. The ditto suit was a fairly informal type of dress clothing, and it was generally worn for business, travel, or street wear.

The early part of the 1800s had been a time of careful dress for men, sometimes called the era of dandies. Dandies were men

THE DANDY

Dandy is a name for a man who pays great attention to dress and fashion and often dresses with a flamboyant style. The term was first used in the late eighteenth century, but became better defined in the early nineteenth century. At first, "dandy" referred to a group of trendsetting young aristocrats in England. Other names for dandies include beaus, mashers, macaronis, fops, and exquisites. Although first used to refer to a flamboyant dresser, by the nineteenth century a dandy was a man who dressed with a careful stylishness. In the twenty-first century the term "dandy" is still used to refer to either a fastidious or a flamboyant dresser.

Dandyism had its roots in the Macaroni Club formed in London, England, in the 1760s by a group of rich young Englishmen who had just returned from a tour of Italy. The Macaronis championed elaborate and exaggerated styles of dress. They loaded themselves down with layer after layer of lace ruffles and gold embroidery and wore knee buckles, striped stockings, and shoes with bright red heels. Some of them sported wigs that were at least a foot high, topped by a tricorne, or three-cornered, hat. In fact, the lyric from the famous American patriotic song "Yankee Doodle": "Stuck a feather in his cap and called it macaroni," refers to these early dandy fashions.

Accessories were critical to the dandy's style. The typical dandy carried a long gold-knobbed, tasseled walking stick and was never seen in public without his bejeweled snuff box, in which he carried chewing tobacco. To ward off bad odors he may have carried an artificial nosegay, a small bunch of flowers, or worn powder or perfume. Many dandies brandished swords with diamond handles and hung two fobs, or pocket watches, from their elegantly tailored waistcoats. These early dandies, many of whom adopted the name "Beau," developed a reputation for grace and coolness. Before long, dandy styles popularized by the English macaronis began migrating to the European continent. In France the *Incroyables* (the

Unbelievables) of the 1790s combined fashionable fantasy garments and English country clothes.

The most famous dandy of all, and the man who truly changed the course of men's fashion, was George Bryan "Beau" Brummell (1778–1840). The son of an English butler who was educated at Oxford, a prestigious university in England, Brummell resisted some of the more flamboyant trends of his day. He dressed simply and plainly, preferring wool and cotton fabrics, carefully tailored jackets, and ankle length, loose-fitting trousers in dark or neutral colors worn with white shirts. A typical outfit for Brummell consisted of a blue woolen tailcoat with brass buttons, buckskin colored pantaloons (loose-fitting trousers), and immaculately polished boots. And he didn't wear a wig or makeup. The only item of elaborate clothing he wore was his necktie—a large bow-tied cravat, a scarf tied around the neck.

Brummell's contribution to fashion was to set a new standard of elegance and ideal of perfection in male dress. He stressed the importance of neatness and cleanliness, as well as refinement and restraint. Brummell took up to five hours to dress every day, though his goal was to make it appear as though he had not. He was one of the first to take regular baths (a custom which was catching on quickly in nineteenth-century Europe), priding himself on the fact that he did not need to wear perfume. It was said that he had three separate hairdressers: one for his forelock, or bangs, one for the hair at the back of his head, and one for his sideburns. He sent his shirts out of town to be washed because he didn't think London laundresses could bleach them white enough.

Beau Brummell's fame and influence long outlived him. Through his friendship with the future British king George IV (1762–1830), he left a lasting mark on English fashion. Though the dandies are long gone, and often mocked in comedies about the period for their excessive manner of dress, men in the West continue to wear trousers and somber colors and to dress themselves in the elegant style set by these fashion pioneers.

who paid careful attention to their clothes and followed the latest trends. Such stylishly dressed men as Englishman George "Beau" Brummell (1778–1840) had a great influence on men's fashions. High-collars, perfectly starched cravats, and tailor-fit jackets, vests, and trousers in complimentary colors were all part of the dandy's look during the first half of the nineteenth century. The perfection of fit that the dandies sought was not reproduced in the first ready-to-wear clothing. Introduced in 1860, the ditto suit offered a loose-fitting ready-to-wear outfit made from the same color and type of fabric. Middle-class and working men quickly adopted the ditto suit as an easy, less-expensive alternative to the expensive tailor-made dress clothes modeled by the dandies. Ready-made clothes soon began to replace tailor-made clothing. By the end of the century, the ditto suit had become the most popular type of everyday suit for most American and European men.

FOR MORE INFORMATION

Bigelow, Marybelle S. *Fashion in History: Western Dress, Prehistoric to Present.* Minneapolis, MN: Burgess Publishing, 1970.

[*See also* **Volume 4, 1930–45: Men's Suits**]

Dresses

The simple answer to the question about what women wore during the nineteenth century is a dress. There were, however, enormous changes in the size, shape, and decoration of women's dresses during the century. At the beginning of the century women abandoned the heavy garments of the previous century and wore the lightest, sheerest of dresses, such as the robe en chemise, modeled after styles worn by ancient Greeks. The muslin or silk fabric of these dresses was so delicate that it could not support pockets, so women began to carry pocketbooks. Most commonly white or light in color, these dresses had short sleeves, high waists, and long, straight skirts. Women did wear light corsets beneath them, but the dresses were meant to show off more of the female form than ever before in Europe or America.

Merely two decades into the century, women's dresses became heavier and more ornate. The early natural silhouette was transformed into a dramatic hourglass shape accentuated by a tightly corseted waist, a full bell-shaped skirt, puffy gigot sleeves, and floppy hats. The skirts of dresses were expanded even further with wire-hoop or whalebone crinolines. By 1860, skirts were so wide that fashionably dressed women could no longer fit through doorways. During the last decades of the century, women's dresses changed shape yet again. The shoulders were accentuated and the skirt's fullness was pushed to the rear and supported by the padding of a bustle, a rear support for a skirt.

The appearance of machine-made trimmings during the century greatly influenced the decoration of dresses, which became ever more colorful and heavily embellished with lace, pleats, ruffles, bows, and other ornament. Some evening dresses held as much as seventy yards of thick ruffles. In addition, newly invented dyes introduced colors to fabrics such as bright pink, turquoise, and yellow, and dresses combined these in striking color combinations. As the century ended, women's dresses continued to change as women's place in society began to shift towards more liberty.

FOR MORE INFORMATION

Costume Illustration: The Nineteenth Century. Introduction by James Laver. London, England: Victoria and Albert Museum, 1947.

Fletcher, Marion. *Female Costume in the Nineteenth Century.* (National Gallery Booklets) Melbourne: Oxford University Press, 1966.

Gibbs-Smith, Charles H. *The Fashionable Lady in the 19th Century.* London, England: Her Majesty's Stationery Office, 1960.

Fur

The most ancient humans created the garments they wore from materials that were around them, and it is likely that animal furs were one of the earliest materials used in the making of clothes. Fur clothing is not only soft, warm, and durable, but has often been a sign of wealth and rank in society. During the late nineteenth and early twentieth centuries it became fashionable for both men and women to wear fur and fur trimmed coats, hats, dresses, and other accessories. Even the top hat, one of the most commonly worn items of the 1800s, could be made from beaver fur. This popularity continued until the 1960s, when some people began to protest the deaths of animals for clothing. They stopped wearing it themselves and protested against those who did.

During the Middle Ages (c. 500–c. 1500) fur was widely used in Europe as a luxurious trim worn by noblemen on cloaks, hats, and tunics to show their wealth and importance. Men also wore fur coats, almost always with the fur on the inside, as a soft, warm lining. Fur was so popular that the buying and selling of furs became a major part of European economies, and a major reason behind the exploration of the New World. In the late eighteenth-century United States, men like John Jacob Astor became millionaires in the fur trade, shipping thousands of beaver furs to Europe to be pressed into thick, durable felt for hats.

During the late 1800s, France, the capital of the Western fashion world, developed a friendly alliance with Russia. The Tsar, or ruler, of Russia visited Paris, to the delight of cheering crowds, and all over Europe people took an interest in Russian styles, especially in the wearing of fur. Hats, scarves, and muffs were made of fur. Cloth coats and dresses were trimmed with fur collars, cuffs, and bands around the hem. Men wore ankle-length coats made of buffalo and beaver, and women wore coats made of Russian sable and Hudson Bay seal. The seal coat was the first fur coat to be worn with the fur on the outside to show off its beauty and texture. This trend, started in 1840, spread throughout Europe and by the mid-nineteenth century had become customary throughout the Western world. As fur became something to display on the outside of garments, sometimes two different types of fur were used so that the different furs provided a contrast. Even whole small animals, such as foxes, were used, including the head and feet, to make a fur wrap. A single whole animal skin, called a stole, could be worn around the shoulders or many whole animals could be sewn together to make a large wrap.

During the early part of the twentieth century, the manufacture of the automobile gave fur clothing another boost. Cars were open and driving could be quite cold and messy. Many men and women wore long coats made of sturdy fur such as raccoon, lynx, or sheepskin to protect them on windy drives.

The French House of Paquin, founded in late 1891, was an important designer of fur fashions. Madame Isidore Paquin not only designed many fur and fur-trimmed garments, but also developed a method of treating furs to make them softer and more comfortable. Some fashion experts said that every well-dressed woman of the early 1900s had a fur-trimmed Paquin coat.

Even during the 1800s, many people protested that wearing fur was cruel to animals and even barbaric. By the 1960s the number of people who felt this way had grown. In addition, fabric manufacturers had developed attractive "fake" furs that imitated the look, warmth, and softness of fur. During the late 1900s and early 2000s, many people chose to wear imitation fur instead of real fur.

FOR MORE INFORMATION

Crawford, M.D.C. *The Ways of Fashion.* New York: G.P. Putnam's Sons, 1941.

Municchi, Anna. *Ladies in Furs, 1900–1940.* Hollywood, CA: Costume and Fashion Press, 1996.

Gigot Sleeves

Gigot is the French word for the back leg of an animal, especially of a lamb or sheep. The gigot sleeve, also called the leg-of-mutton sleeve, was named for its resemblance to a sheep's hind leg: wide at the top and narrow at the bottom. With a large puff of material at the shoulder, gigot sleeves tapered sharply at the elbow to fit closely along the lower arm. This dramatic style of sleeve was first seen on women's dresses in the sixteenth century but became a very popular style during the late 1820s and early 1830s, a romantic period that favored flamboyant styles. The gigot or leg-of-mutton sleeve came into style again during the 1890s as part of the fashionable hourglass figure, for which women were supposed to be wide at the shoulders and bust, narrow at the waist, and wide at the hips.

The wide puffed gigot sleeve was showy and stylish but not very practical. In order to hold the fabric out in a large balloon shape at the top of the arm, whalebone strips were sewn into the sleeve.

For very large gigots, padding and even hoops were used to keep the shape of the sleeve. All these additions to the large sleeve made it hard for women to use their arms, or even to enter narrow doorways. Some fashion critics considered the style so ridiculous they nicknamed the gigots "imbecile sleeves." However, during the periods in which they were popular, many women's dresses featured the wide sleeves, and even little girls and boys under six years old wore dresses with miniature versions of the puffy gigot sleeve.

FOR MORE INFORMATION

Hansen, Henny H. *Costumes and Styles: The Evolution of Fashion from Early Egypt to the Present.* New York: E.P. Dutton, 1973.

[*See also* **Volume 3, Sixteenth Century: Sleeves**]

The dramatic gigot sleeve was first seen on women's dresses in the sixteenth century. The sleeve soon became so large that it was sometimes difficult for women to fit through narrow doorways. *Reproduced by permission of © Bettmann/CORBIS.*

Kashmir Shawls

Indian textiles began flooding European markets in the seventeenth century with the founding of the Dutch East India Company in 1597 and the English East India Company in 1600. This early trade provided the foundation for the great popularity of Kashmir shawls among fashionable European women in the late eighteenth and early nineteenth centuries. Kashmir shawls had been woven since the fifteenth century, but Europeans first became acquainted with them in the seventeenth century.

Kashmir shawls were made of fine cashmere, pashima, and shah tus wools, made from the soft hair of Tibetan mountain goats living in the high altitudes of the Himalayan Mountains. Indian women spun the fleece into yarn and one or two men worked between two to three years weaving the yarn into a shawl. Undyed shawls ranged in color from light cream to grey or brown. To produce more vibrant shawls, yarns were dyed with natural pigments or silk thread was woven into the shawl. Patterns called boteh, which means flower but the pattern is recognized as paisley in the West, were woven into the shawls named kani. Shawls with embroidered patterns were called amli. The great skill and long time it took to make each Kashmir shawl made them very expensive. In the early nineteenth century a Kashmir shawl was as expensive as a twentieth-century mink coat.

Despite the high price of these shawls, demand increased rapidly among European women. Recognizing the potential for profit, European textile manufacturers began to make imitation Kashmir shawls in factories located throughout Europe. Power loom woven shawls cost one-tenth the price of handmade Kashmir shawls. Paisley, Scotland had such high success producing imitation Kashmir shawls that the traditional Indian boteh pattern became known in the West as paisley.

Although the huge supply of imitation shawls damaged the popularity of Kashmir shawls, it was another fashion trend that ended the demand for these shawls. The large Kashmir shawls covered the hoops of crinoline skirts perfectly on chilly days. But the 1870 fashion for the bustled skirt, which made the back of a women's dress into a decorative bump, would be completely covered by a Kashmir shawl. Wanting to show off their bustles, women stopped wearing the shawls.

FOR MORE INFORMATION

Askari, Nasreen, and Liz Arthur. *Uncut Cloth: Saris, Shawls, and Sashes.* London, England: Merrell Holberton, 1999.

Goswamy, B. N., and Kalyan Krishna. *Indian Costumes in the Collection of the Calico Museum of Textiles.* Ahmedabad, India: D. S. Mehta, 1993.

[*See also* **Volume 1, India: Chadar**]

Pelisse

Named for the Latin word *pellicus,* meaning "made of skin," the pelisse was a loose cape made of fur, or made of velvet or satin and lined or trimmed with fur. Popular during the late eighteenth and early nineteenth centuries, the pelisse was a warm outer garment, commonly worn by women and children. The design is thought to be an example of Middle Eastern influence on European and American styles.

A kind of combination cloak and coat, the pelisse usually had a large collar, though some had hoods to give even more protection from the weather. The length of the pelisse varied from ankle length to hip length, and the fashionable length changed from year to year, the way women's skirt hemlines did during the mid-twentieth century. Most pelisses had slits in the front for the hands to reach through, but some were designed with short or long sleeves, making them resemble a loose, flowing coat. Some of the sleeved pelisses were fitted more closely to the body and looked almost like an overdress.

A variation of the warm fur-lined pelisse was the pelisse robe, which was worn by women indoors. Usually made of muslin (sheer cotton fabric) or other light material, the pelisse robe was designed in much the same way as the outdoor pelisse, as a cape with a collar, worn over the dress for modesty and warmth.

FOR MORE INFORMATION

Bigelow, Marybelle S. *Fashion in History: Western Dress, Prehistoric to Present.* Minneapolis, MN: Burgess Publishing, 1970.

Yarwood, Doreen. *Fashion in the Western World: 1500–1900.* New York: Drama Book Publishers, 1992.

Tennis Costume

The nineteenth century saw phenomenal growth in sporting activities, for women as well as for men, particularly between 1870 and 1900. All manner of new sports came into favor, and it was impossible to practice them with any comfort in the formal dress of the day. Clothes had to be adapted accordingly, but progress was slow, especially for women.

Lawn tennis became a popular sport in England and the United States in the 1870s. However, women's clothes made few conces-

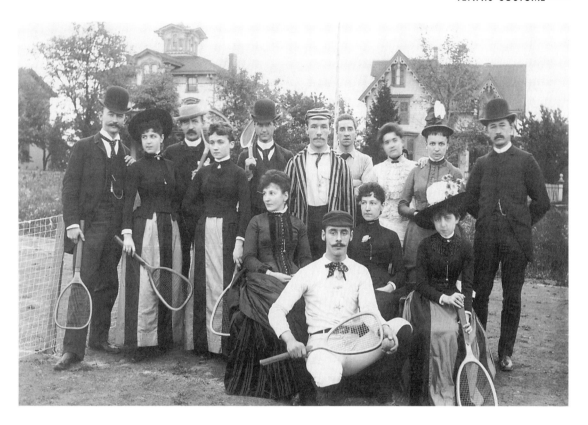

sions to the sport. Women played in dresses with high-necked bodices, layers of petticoats, and floor-length skirts that made it virtually impossible to bend over to retrieve tennis balls. As a result, by the 1880s special tennis aprons, often beautifully embroidered and furnished with large pockets to accommodate the balls, had become fashionable tennis attire for women. Maud Watson, the winner of the first ladies singles championship held at Wimbledon in England in 1884, is said to have provoked much gossip by running around the court in an ankle-length white dress, driving and volleying with great skill.

Men's clothes were more adaptable to sports. Typical tennis attire for a man included knickerbockers, loose-fitting short pants gathered at the knee, or cream or white flannel trousers with long-sleeved flannel shirts, short silk ties, knitted hose, and kerchiefs or sashes around the waist. A low-laced early version of the tennis shoe was also coming into fashion. Paintings from the late nineteenth century depict British men playing in shirtsleeves, a shirt without a coat, or with trouser hems turned up above the ankles,

Lawn tennis became a popular sport in England and the United States in the 1870s. Women's restrictive clothing made few concessions to the sport, whereas men's clothes allowed for more freedom of movement. *Reproduced by permission of © Bettmann/ CORBIS.*

a sign that standards of etiquette were relaxing to allow for ease of movement.

FOR MORE INFORMATION

Setnik, Linda. *Victorian Costume for Ladies.* Atglen, PA: Schiffer Publishing, 2000.

Ulseth, Hazel, and Helen Shannon. *Victorian Fashions.* Cumberland, MD: Hobby House Press, 1989.

Nineteenth-Century Headwear

Over the course of the nineteenth century hairstyles and headwear changed quite dramatically from the styles of the previous century. At the beginning of the century, both men and women fashioned their hair in styles like those worn in ancient Greece and Rome. Women wore the Titus cut popularized at the end of the eighteenth century and in a variety of braided styles. Men clipped their hair short and brushed it forward from the crown over the forehead in a style similar to those worn by ancient Greeks and Romans. Over the years, however, men and women created the unique styles for which the nineteenth century is now remembered: men's sideburns and women's ornate topknots, or piles of hair on top of the head.

At the beginning of the century, men, especially young men, clipped off their lovelocks and pigtails to create very short hairstyles that they combed forward over their foreheads. Throughout the century men continued to wear short hair. The variety of styles they chose were distinguished by the middle, side, or lack of a part and the type of face whiskers they wore.

Women's styles concentrated on variations of a topknot with hair framing the face at the temples. At the beginning of the century, women abandoned their huge powdered wigs to twist their hair into Apollo knots and adorn their heads with Greek inspired wreaths, sphendone, jeweled ornaments, flowers, and strands of

At the beginning of the nineteenth century, both men and women fashioned their hair in styles like those worn in ancient Greece and Rome. Women's styles concentrated on variations of a topknot with hair framing the face at the temples. *Reproduced by permission of AP/Wide World Photos.*

pearls. As the century progressed, women's hair continued to be worn swept on top of the head, but the styles became more ornate. Their hair was greased, braided, and twisted into elaborate knots with curled or frizzed hair at the sides. To appear properly groomed and to keep proper care of the hair, women commonly styled their hair twice a day, even if only to put it back into the same shape. Women's hairstyles had become so elaborate by the end of the century that hair was supported with pads and wire, and wigs were back in demand. These elaborate styles provided many poor women with needed money, as they cut their hair and sold it to wigmakers.

The distinct styles of men and women were not worn by children. Small children wore their hair in loose curls with a side part. It was often difficult to tell boys from girls. However, by the teen years girls wore their hair longer and braided it, while boys generally wore their hair loose and shorter.

Both men and women dressed their hair with Macassar oil or perfumed grease. The oil made the hair smell good and kept it in place. One recipe for homemade hair pomade, or perfumed ointment, combined one part lard to five parts strongly scented flowers.

Atop their carefully styled hair both men and women wore a variety of hats. The top hat became an essential accessory for men, and women donned a number of different styles, from tiny bonnets to huge floppy Gainsborough chapeaus, or no hat at all when their hair was decorated with a variety of ornaments from simple flowers to expensive jeweled combs.

FOR MORE INFORMATION

Corson, Richard. *Fashions in Hair: The First Five Thousand Years.* London, England: Peter Owen, 2001.

Trasko, Mary. *Daring Do's: A History of Extraordinary Hair.* New York: Flammarion, 1994.

Apollo Knot

The Apollo knot hairstyle had three essential parts: the front of the hair was combed into a center part; the long hair at the back was piled neatly in a bun on top of the head; and small ringlets fell beside the temples to frame the face. The style reflected the trend in the early nineteenth century to wear Greek-inspired dress styles and hair ornaments called sphendone and wreaths. Women either used their own hair or false hair pieces to create Apollo knots. Sometimes they decorated the front of their Apollo knots with decorative combs.

FOR MORE INFORMATION

Laver, James. *Costume and Fashion: A Concise History.* 4th ed. London, England: Thames and Hudson, 2002.

Payne, Blanche, Geitel Winakor, and Jane Farrell-Beck. *The History of Costume.* 2nd ed. New York: HarperCollins, 1992.

[*See also* **Volume 1, Ancient Greece: Sakkos and Sphendone; Volume 1, Ancient Greece: Wreaths**]

Bowler

The distinctively British bowler is a hard felt hat with a low melon-shaped crown and a rounded brim that turns up at the sides. Known in the United States as a derby hat, the bowler had largely replaced the hard-to-maintain top hat as the headgear of choice for elegant gentlemen in the United States and Europe by the end of the nineteenth century.

The first bowler hat was designed in 1850. Tired of his tall riding hat being yanked off by overhanging tree branches while traveling in his coach, William Coke II, a wealthy British landowner, commissioned the renowned London, England, hatters James and George Lock to design a low-crowned hat. The Locks, who called their creation a Coke hat, sent their design across the Thames River to one of their chief suppliers, William Bowler. Bowler produced a prototype and soon began manufacturing the hat under his own name. The name stuck, perhaps because the hat's bowl-like shape made it easy to remember.

Early bowlers came in gray, brown, or black, with black the most popular color. Brims could also be curled up or straight. First

The distinctively British bowler is a hard felt hat with a low melon-shaped crown and a rounded brim that turns up at the sides.
Reproduced by permission of © Bettmann/CORBIS.

worn for casual occasions, the low-crowned bowler became a popular accompaniment to lounge suits among English men visiting the countryside in the 1860s and a slightly taller-crowned version caught on among tourists in Paris, France. However, the declining popularity of the top hat, which was large and hard to keep clean, resulted in the bowler becoming acceptable as town wear by the turn of the century. The hat shape was eventually adapted for women and children and remained popular with British men until World War II (1939–45). New York governor Alfred E. Smith (1873–1944) helped popularize a brown version of the hat in the United States, where it was called the derby.

Today the bowler hat is widely associated with Great Britain, due to its adoption by several well-known historical and fictional Englishmen. Silent film comedians Charlie Chaplin (1889–1977) and Stan Laurel (1890–1965), and more recently the dashing gentleman spy character, John Steed, of the 1960s television series *The Avengers* (1961–69), all sported bowlers.

FOR MORE INFORMATION

Chenoune, Farid. *A History of Men's Fashion.* Paris, France: Flammarion, 1993.

Robinson, Fred Miller. *The Man in the Bowler Hat: His History and Iconography.* Chapel Hill, NC: University of North Carolina Press, 1993.

[*See also* **Volume 3, Nineteenth Century: Top Hat; Volume 4, 1919–29: Derby**]

Deerstalker Cap

The deerstalker was a type of cap favored by deer hunters and other sportsmen in nineteenth-century England. The deerstalker became especially fashionable between 1870 and 1890, when sports clothes became a more prominent feature of men's dress. The cap was often worn with Norfolk jackets and knicker-bockers, short loosely fitting pants gathered at the knee, and considered an essential element of the Victorian (relating to the times of Britain's Queen Victoria [1819–1901]) hunting ensemble. Also called a "fore and aft," the deerstalker was distinguished by its front and back visors. Large exterior earflaps could be tied on top or allowed to cover the ears for warmth. The cap was usually made of checked material, typically sportsman's tweed or cloth. The crown was lined with scarlet poplin and was reversible.

More than a sportsman's cap, the deer-stalker is commonly associated with British writer Arthur Conan Doyle's (1859–1930) fictional detective Sherlock Holmes. It became such a recognized symbol of Holmes thanks to illustrator Sidney Paget (1860–1908). Although Doyle never referred to his character Sherlock Holmes as wearing a deerstalker, Paget drew the cap on Holmes's head in several stories, perhaps because he himself wore one. Actors playing Holmes on stage and screen have consistently referred to Paget's drawings as a model. Another famous fictional deerstalker wearer was Holden Caulfield, the protagonist of author J. D. Salinger's (1919–) famous novel *The Catcher in the Rye* (1951).

The deerstalker cap became especially fashionable when sports clothes became a more prominent feature of men's dress. The deerstalker is commonly associated with the fictional detective Sherlock Holmes. *Reproduced by permission of Getty Images.*

FOR MORE INFORMATION

Chenoune, Farid. *A History of Men's Fashion.* Paris, France: Flammarion, 1993.

Harrison, Michael. *The History of the Hat.* London, England: Herbert Jenkins, 1960.

Ulseth, Hazel, and Helen Shannon. *Victorian Fashions.* Cumberland, MD: Hobby House Press, 1989.

Gainsborough Chapeau

The Gainsborough chapeau was a women's hat style that was first popularized at the turn of the nineteenth century. Based on the hats often seen on the ladies painted by famous British portrait artist Thomas Gainsborough (1727–1788), the Gainsborough chapeau was a large hat with a wide brim, trimmed with feathers, ribbons, and flowers. Made of velvet, felt, or straw, Gainsborough hats were big and showy, and they sat high up on the elaborate hairstyles worn by most women of the day. Very popular at the end of the eighteenth century, the large Gainsborough chapeau became fashionable again at the end of the nineteenth century atop the high pompadour styles of the Gibson girls.

Woman wearing a Gainsborough chapeau, a large hat with a wide brim, trimmed with feathers, ribbons, and flowers. *Reproduced by permission of © CORBIS.*

Gainsborough hats were also called picture hats, garden hats, and cartwheels, because of their large size and the elaborate decorations that adorned them. These decorations usually included large feathers, and even whole stuffed birds. During the early 1900s, when the Gainsborough chapeau reached its largest size, some countries passed laws forbidding the use of certain bird feathers on the hats to prevent whole species from being killed off.

Rather than sitting down over the head, the Gainsborough style was to frame the head by sitting up above the hair. A cloth band below the brim of the hat fitted over the top of the hairstyle, and long hatpins were stuck through this band to hold the hat on the head. Hatpins grew so long that they sometimes poked people walking by. Some states in the United States passed laws limiting the length of hatpins for public safety.

FOR MORE INFORMATION

Bigelow, Marybelle S. *Fashion in History: Western Dress, Prehistoric to Present.* Minneapolis, MN: Burgess Publishing, 1970.

Mustaches

Men have always had the option of growing facial hair over their upper lip, but in terms of fashion the nineteenth century was the golden age of mustaches. Beginning about midcentury, a wide variety of mustache styles became popular across Europe and North America, and they remained so into the 1900s.

The nineteenth century saw the return of more assertively masculine styles of dress and grooming throughout the Western world. Much of the craze for mustaches began in the military ranks of various countries. The French armed forces, the Prussian guard, and the British Hussars, or light cavalry officers, were all required to wear mustaches.

In England mustache fashion spread from the uniformed ranks to the general public in the aftermath of the Crimean War (1853–56), which pitted Britain and France against Russia. Soldiers who had let their whiskers grow on the battlefield brought the look home to England, starting a trend that swept Europe. The drooping "walrus" mustache was one of the popular styles associated with the British army. Other mustaches were inspired by political and military leaders of the century. Long sidewhiskers that merged into a mustache became known as a "Franz Josef" in honor of the Austrian emperor who ruled from 1848

The nineteenth century was the golden age of mustaches and sideburns, and there were many popular styles of each. *Reproduced by permission of AP/Wide World Photos.*

to 1916. A waxed mustache turned up at the ends was dubbed a "Kaiser" after Kaiser Wilhelm II (1859–1941) of Germany, who ruled from 1888 to 1918. In the United States a similar mustache that curled upwards at the ends, called a "handlebar" after the curved steering bar on a bicycle, became quite popular in the 1890s.

By the close of the century, the mustache was falling out of favor among the style-conscious. American illustrator Charles Dana Gibson (1867–1944) created the popular Gibson girls in the 1890s, which were a good measure of popular fashions of the times, and showed the fashionable escorts as clean-shaven. Mustaches remained quite popular, however, chiefly among older and professional men, well into the twentieth century.

FOR MORE INFORMATION

Byrde, Penelope. *Nineteenth Century Fashion.* London, England: B. T. Batsford, 1992.

Corson, Richard. *Fashions in Hair: The First Five Thousand Years.* London, England: Peter Owen, 2001.

Sideburns

Sideburns, or facial hair extending past the ear and along the cheek, became a popular male hairstyle during the nineteenth century in Europe and America. Historian Richard Corson identified sideburns, or side-whiskers, as the fashion distinguishing the nineteenth century from other periods, noting that "the timid sproutings [of hair] of the early years had flourished and often developed into flowing, luxuriant growths, frequently unaccompanied by any beard or mustache." During the century men grew a huge variety of sideburn styles. Unlike other periods, "the question," according to Corson, "was no longer whether or not to wear whiskers but simply what kind."

At the turn of the century, European and American men, except military men, were generally clean-shaven. Side-whiskers on American men's faces were first observed during the War of 1812. By the middle of the century, these whiskers worn with a clean-shaven chin were called side-whiskers or Dundrearies, after a whiskered character named Lord Dundreary in the popular play *Our*

American Cousin (1858). But it was during the American Civil War (1861–65), when men in combat often went weeks without shaving, that side-whiskers became most popular. The Union army general Ambrose Burnside (1824–1881), later governor of Rhode Island, was known for his prominent side-whiskers, and the style became known as burnsides. A less dramatic set of side-whiskers came to be known as sideburns, sidebar whiskers, or sideboards.

By midcentury men of many professions wore unique styles of sideburns. In some professions where beards and mustaches were not allowed, such as organized team sports, one of the few ways men were allowed to express themselves was to grow long sideburns. Future U.S. president Theodore Roosevelt (1858–1919), while an undergraduate at Harvard in the late 1870s, wore very heavy sideburns called mutton chops or lamb chops, which became popular late in the nineteenth century. Incidentally, the common American saying "to bust someone's chops," introduced in the 1880s, meant to hit someone in their sideburned face.

After 1900, sideburns fell out of fashion. However, during the 1960s they returned to fashion, made popular again by such rock stars as British band The Beatles and the singer James Brown.

FOR MORE INFORMATION

Corson, Richard. *Fashions in Hair: The First Five Thousand Years.* London, England: Peter Owen, 2001.

Flexner, Stuart Berg. *Listening to America: An Illustrated History of Words and Phrases from Our Lively and Splendid Past.* New York: Touchstone, 1982.

Spoon Bonnets

Women first began wearing the cloth head coverings called bonnets during the 1700s, but they are most strongly identified with the nineteenth century. Designed to protect the head and hair from sun, wind, and rain, bonnets differed from hats because they did not sit on top of the head, but were fitted around the head, usually tying under the chin with long, decorative ribbons. Like hats, bonnets had a brim around the crown in the front, but sewn to the back,

A red spoon bonnet in the lower, left corner. Designed to protect the head and hair from sun, wind, and rain, bonnets did not sit on top of the head, but fit around the head, usually tying under the chin with long, decorative ribbons. *Reproduced by permission of © Historical Picture Archive/CORBIS.*

instead of a brim, was a piece of fabric called a curtain, which protected the wearer's neck.

A bonnet's primary function was to cover a woman's head and even part of her face, both for modesty and to protect it from the weather. However, bonnets were also highly decorative fashion accessories. One of the most ornate of all bonnets was the spoon bonnet, which was introduced during the early 1860s. One of the most popular women's hats of the American Civil War (1861–65) era, the spoon bonnet had a wide front brim that rose straight up from the crown, giving the bonnet the shape of a shallow spoon. While providing little protection from sun or rain, the underside of the tall brim could be decorated with ruffles, lace, bows, and silk flowers, making the spoon bonnet frame the wearer's face prettily. Because it had little use except as decoration, the spoon bonnet was largely worn by wealthy women, or young women who wanted to wear the latest fashions.

The spoon bonnet was the last nineteenth-century bonnet that was styled to cover the head. By the 1880s, as women's hairstyles became more elaborate, few women wanted to cover them up, and they began to wear smaller bonnets which sat on top of the head, more like a traditional hat. Finally the bonnet disappeared to be replaced by modern hats whose only function was decoration.

FOR MORE INFORMATION

Langley, Susan. *Vintage Hats & Bonnets 1770–1970.* Paducah, KY: Collector Books, 1997.

Top Hat

Introduced during the early 1800s, the top hat became the most common men's hat of the nineteenth century. Worn by men of all classes, for all occasions, at any time of day, the top hat was a narrow-brimmed silk hat with a tall, straight crown and a flat top. Formal, dramatic, and imposing, the top hat represented much of the spirit of the late eighteenth and nineteenth centuries, in which middle class and wealthy Europeans focused on elegance and formality in their dress and manners. The century even saw the first rabbit pulled out of a top hat by French magician Louis Conte in 1814.

The top hat had been preceded by other tall-crowned hats, most made of beaver fur felt and called beaver hats. When British hatmaker John Hetherington first wore his new creation, a tall, straight-crowned hat made of shiny silk, into the streets of London in 1800, passersby were shocked at first, but soon the top hat caught on. By the 1820s top hats were seen everywhere. The height and shape varied somewhat through the century, but the tall hat became the symbol of the nineteenth-century man.

The Romantic Movement of the late eighteenth and early nineteenth centuries in France, Germany, England, and America established an emotional, romantic style in literature, art, and clothing, and top hat designs reflected this flamboyant period with very tall crowns that tapered to wide tops and dashingly curved brims. Hats grew so tall that in 1823 a Frenchman named Antoine Gibus invented a collapsible top hat. Called an opera hat, it could be folded flat at the theater. During the next two decades, top hats became so tall and straight that they were given the name stovepipes. American millionaire J. P. Morgan (1837–1913) had a special limousine made with a high roof so that he could wear his hat in the car. Even women joined the fashion, as popular women's riding clothes included a top hat with an attached veil.

The 1900s brought a less formal attitude towards dress, and the top hat faded from popularity, to be replaced by shorter, less stately hats such as derbies and bowlers.

Introduced during the early 1800s, the top hat became the most common men's hat of the nineteenth century. *Reproduced by permission of the Kobal Collection.*

Top hats came to be used only for very formal occasions. A remnant of the age of the top hat can be found in the English language slang "high-hat," meaning conceited or snobbish.

FOR MORE INFORMATION

Henderson, Debbie B. *The Top Hat: An Illustrated History of Its Styling and Manufacture.* Yellow Springs, OH: Wild Goose Press, 2000.

Wigs

Wigs, false hairpieces that are worn over or attached to the natural hair of the wearer, have been fashion accessories for many centuries. The nineteenth century did not see the widespread use of elaborate wigs that had marked previous eras. Still, false hair remained popular during the 1800s, mainly for women who wished to achieve fashionable hairstyles that required abundant curls.

Both men and women had commonly worn wigs during the 1700s, but by the end of the century the popularity of the elaborately powdered and styled wig was beginning to fade. At the start of the nineteenth century much of fashionable society began to be fascinated with the styles of ancient Greece and Rome. Many men trimmed their hair in a short, informal cut, in the style of Roman generals, while some women adopted a classic Greco-Roman women's style of masses of curls, loosely bound up on the head. Those who did not have enough curls of their own, added false pieces of hair called *cachefolies* (French for "hidden foolishness") to add the necessary volume of hair.

During the 1860s wigs again became popular for women, as hairstyles with masses of long ringlets came into fashion. For those women who could not afford full wigs, partial wigs were available to add hair where it was needed. Wigs were costly, and women who needed money could cut their hair and sell it to wigmakers, the way the literary character Jo March did in the 1868 novel *Little Women,* by Louisa May Alcott (1832–1888).

FOR MORE INFORMATION

Bigelow, Marybelle S. *Fashion in History: Apparel in the Western World.* Minneapolis, MN: Burgess Publishing, 1970.

Payne, Blanche, Geitel Winakor, and Jane Farrell-Beck. *The History of Costume.* 2nd ed. New York: HarperCollins, 1992.

Nineteenth-Century Body Decorations

Both men and women wore an abundance of accessories to appear fashionable during the nineteenth century. Women's accessories reflected what time of day it was. During the day, women wore elbow-length gloves, and carried fans, small purses called reticules, eyeglasses on long handles, and parasols. In the evening, women wore longer gloves and jewelry. Although women wore simple necklaces and earrings at the beginning of the century, they began to display their wealth by wearing more and more bracelets, necklaces, small rings, earrings, and brooches as the century wore on. Men's accessories were simpler. No matter the time of day, men carried ebony canes, or thin bamboo canes in the summer, and attached pocket watches with a variety of fobs and seals to the right side of their waistcoats.

Cleanliness became fashionable in this century. Though during past centuries in Europe bathing had been frowned upon, the practice now became more appealing. The first dandy, or fashionable young man, the Englishman George "Beau" Brummell (1778–1840), prided himself on being clean enough to go without perfume. His example influenced many, including the future British king George IV (1762–1830), who began washing themselves regularly and carefully maintaining their cleanliness throughout the day.

Among the upper classes, white skin remained desirable, especially for women. White skin identified a person's status because only the wealthy could afford to remain idle and indoors all day long. Women protected themselves from the sun with parasols and dusted their faces with white powder to lighten their complexions.

FOR MORE INFORMATION

Bigelow, Marybelle S. *Fashion in History: Apparel in the Western World.* Minneapolis, MN: Burgess Publishing, 1970.

Laver, James. *Costume and Fashion: A Concise History.* 4th ed. London, England: Thames and Hudson, 2002.

Lister, Margot. *Costume: An Illustrated Survey from Ancient Times to the Twentieth Century.* London, England: Herbert Jenkins, 1967.

Payne, Blanche, Geitel Winakor, and Jane Farrell-Beck. *The History of Costume.* 2nd ed. New York: HarperCollins, 1992.

Ascots

Man wearing red ascot. The ascot was a wide scarf-like necktie most popular with well-dressed British gentlemen in the second half of the nineteenth century. *Painting by Paul Cezanne. Reproduced by permission of © Kimbell Art Museum/CORBIS.*

The ascot was a wide scarf-like necktie popular with well-dressed British gentlemen in the second half of the nineteenth century. It was originally named after a racetrack, Ascot Heath in England, where the style was popularized by fashionable spectators attending the Royal Ascot, an annual four-day horse race initiated by Queen Anne (1665–1714) in 1711. An ascot is sometimes called a cravat, though this word originated as a general term for any style of neckwear. In the United States the word ascot is synonymous with cravat.

Commonly worn for business in the late nineteenth and early twentieth centuries, the ascot was considered more formal than the "four-in-hand" knotted tie, which resembles the modern necktie and became popular among men in the late nineteenth century. The ascot was generally made of black satin and fastened in the center with a jeweled stickpin. It was usually self-tied and might be puffed out in the center front and called a puffed ascot. It was typically worn with a winged collar tuxedo shirt. The ascot was similar in style to two other cravats of the period: the cross-over neckcloth of the 1840s, which was a simple scarf loosely tied around the neck, and the octagon of the 1860s, which featured four tabs arranged above a pin positioned at the center front of the neck.

The ascot reached the height of popularity during the 1890s, when fashionable men began to adopt more colorful styles in neck-wear. It fell out of favor at the start of the 1900s when the bow tie came into fashion. In the twenty-first century the ascot is rarely worn except with very formal morning wear, to weddings, or at the Royal Ascot races. However, yachtsmen, jetsetters, or those trying to convey an aristocratic attitude continue to wear ascots for other occasions.

FOR MORE INFORMATION

Byrde, Penelope. *Nineteenth Century Fashion.* London, England: B. T. Batsford, 1992.

Ulseth, Hazel, and Helen Shannon. *Victorian Fashions.* Cumberland, MD: Hobby House Press, 1989.

Brooch

A brooch was a pin featuring a large central cut jewel sur-rounded by diamonds or pearls. Women fastened brooches to the necklines of their dresses. At the beginning of the century, women pinned a brooch at the center of their scooped necklines near their breasts or attached a brooch to a ribbon tied tightly around their neck. By the end of the century, however, women covered more of their chests and used brooches to hold their collars in place at the base of their necks.

FOR MORE INFORMATION

Bigelow, Marybelle S. *Fashion in History: Apparel in the Western World.* Minneapolis, MN: Burgess Publishing, 1970.

Payne, Blanche, Geitel Winakor, and Jane Farrell-Beck. *The History of Costume.* 2nd ed. New York: HarperCollins, 1992.

Fobs and Seals

Fobs and seals decorated the waists of fashionable men during the early nineteenth century, continuing a trend that started in the late eighteenth century. Fobs were short straps, ribbons, tassels, or chains. A fob attached to a watch carried in

the pocket of a waistcoat on the man's right side. Seals were engraved gold or other metal medallions attached to fobs, used for marking a person's signature impression in sealing wax for important documents or other correspondence, or purely for ornamentation. The fad for single or clusters of fobs and seals was replaced by the end of the century with a simpler fashion: the display of the pocketwatch chain. Men's main ornamentation during the later years of the nineteenth century was a draped pocketwatch chain hanging across their buttoned waistcoat or vest.

Fobs were short straps, ribbons, tassels, or chains. Reproduced by permission of © Royalty-Free/ CORBIS.

FOR MORE INFORMATION

Bigelow, Marybelle S. *Fashion in History: Apparel in the Western World.* Minneapolis, MN: Burgess Publishing, 1970.

Laver, James. *Costume and Fashion: A Concise History.* 4th ed. London, England: Thames and Hudson, 2002.

Lister, Margot. *Costume: An Illustrated Survey from Ancient Times to the Twentieth Century.* London, England: Herbert Jenkins, 1967.

Payne, Blanche, Geitel Winakor, and Jane Farrell-Beck. *The History of Costume.* 2nd ed. New York: HarperCollins, 1992.

Gloves

Some form of gloves, garments that cover the hands by encasing each finger in fabric or leather, have been worn for protection and warmth for thousands of years. However, their use as a fashion accessory took hold during the 1500s when famous women, such as Elizabeth I (1533–1603) of England, began wearing elbow-length gloves as a part of formal clothing. Gloves continued to gain popularity, and by the 1800s they had become an important part of the everyday wardrobe for both women and men.

Napoleon Bonaparte (1769–1821) and his wife Josephine (1763–1814), the Emperor and Empress of France, introduced the nineteenth-century fashion of wearing gloves. In 1806, the emperor was said to own 240 pairs of gloves, and his wife, who did not think her hands were attractive, wore gloves for every social occasion. Dress styles during that time had short, puffed sleeves, and women, following Empress Josephine's example, covered their bare arms with long gloves that reached almost to the shoulder. Gloves were usually white or ivory-colored and made of silk, lace, or kid, leather made from the skin of baby goats. They often had many buttons to help them fit around the arm and wrist.

As the century progressed, styles grew more modest. Dress sleeves became longer, and gloves, still considered a necessity for well-dressed women, became shorter. Women of the mid- to late 1800s wore wrist-length gloves during the day, even indoors. Since evening dress sleeves were often shorter, longer gloves were worn to cover the arms modestly. It was considered almost indecent for a lady to put on or remove her gloves in public.

Gloves were an important accessory for nineteenth-century men as well, and were worn at every social occasion. The well-dressed

In the 1800s gloves were usually white or ivory-colored and made of silk, lace, or leather. They often reached all the way up to a woman's sleeve, covering her arm. *Reproduced by permission of © Historical Picture Archive/ CORBIS.*

man of the late 1800s never removed his gloves, whether dancing at a ball or relaxing at home.

FOR MORE INFORMATION

Bigelow, Marybelle S. *Fashion in History: Western Dress, Prehistoric to Present.* Minneapolis, MN: Burgess Publishing, 1970.

Yarwood, Doreen. *Fashion in the Western World: 1500–1900.* New York: Drama Book Publishers, 1992.

The single lens eyeglass, or monocle, was introduced in the eighteenth century but attained its greatest popularity in nineteenth-century Europe. It came to be known as an emblem of aristocratic arrogance. *Reproduced by permission of © Hulton-Deutsch Collection/CORBIS.*

Monocle

The single lens eyeglass, or monocle, was introduced in the eighteenth century but attained its greatest popularity in nineteenth-century Europe as an emblem of aristocratic arrogance. Often carried purely for dramatic effect, the monocle was usually worn around the neck on a string, ribbon, or chain, and used to peer down on others with an air of superiority, and when placed on the eye, a person was forced to squint in an awkward manner to hold it in place.

First developed in Germany during the 1700s, and originally called an eye ring, the monocle soon spread to Austria thanks to an enterprising young optics student named J. F. Voigtlander, who started making them in Vienna around 1814. The fashion quickly caught on in England and Russia as well, where the first monocle wearers were men in society's upper classes. Many of these early monocles were framed with metal, tortoiseshell, or horn. More elaborate monocles were made of solid gold and studded with gems.

Monocles went in and out of fashion throughout the 1800s. The typical 1860s dandy, a nickname for a fashionable man, wore loud checked trousers and a monocle, for example. Even during the height of its appeal, the monocle was never regarded as an effective solution for people's vision problems and was only rarely fitted with a real corrective lens. Monocles fell out of favor in much of western Europe and the United States during World War I (1914–18) when they became associated with enemy German military officers who were often depicted wearing them.

FOR MORE INFORMATION

Chenoune, Farid. *A History of Men's Fashion.* Paris, France: Flammarion, 1993.

Rosenthal, J. William. *Spectacles and Other Vision Aids.* Novato, CA: Norman Publishing, 1994.

Pocketbook

Small, handheld bags used to hold money and other necessities, pocketbooks, also called purses, reticules, or handbags, have been an important fashion accessory for women since the late 1700s. People had used small leather or fabric pouches for money and valuables long before that, but those purses had been carried either by men only or by both genders equally. However, from the 1790s through the 1820s, it became fashionable for women to wear simple dresses made of thin, lightweight material. Before this, women had worn full skirts made of yards of heavy materials in which it was easy to hide many pockets to hold such necessities as money, keys, or cosmetics. The lightweight, silky fabrics that became popular at the turn of the nineteenth century would not support deep pockets, so women began to carry small handbags to hold the things they needed. They filled these bags so full that they soon became the object of jokes and ridicule.

Between the early 1800s and the early 1900s, reticules developed from small, drawstring bags made of fabric, with handles to hang over the arm, into pocketbooks with metal frames and snap closures. The first pocketbooks had been made flat and shaped like envelopes. They were closed with ribbon ties and placed in the pocket. Later however, the names pocketbook and purse were both used for any women's handbag. Pocketbooks were made of fabric, leather, or metal mesh attached to a circular metal frame and closed with a metal snap. Pocketbooks made of beaded fabric became popular for eveningwear during the late 1800s.

By the 1910s and 1920s, women's clothing again became lighter, and pocketbooks became a standard accessory, carried by most women at all times. During later decades, they became bigger and sturdier and were usually made of leather, almost like a small suitcase.

FOR MORE INFORMATION

Bigelow, Marybelle S. *Fashion in History: Western Dress, Prehistoric to Present.* Minneapolis, MN: Burgess Publishing, 1970.

Haertig, Evelyn. *Most Beautiful Purses.* Carmel, CA: Gallery Graphic Press, 1990.

Yarwood, Doreen. *Fashion in the Western World: 1500–1900.* New York: Drama Book Publishers, 1992.

Nineteenth-Century Footwear

Men and women living in the nineteenth century enjoyed a variety of foot covering choices. Men's styles were visible beneath their trousers or breeches, but women's long gowns hid their shoes from sight. Men began to wear different styles of heavy boots during the day. Many of these boot styles were popularized by European military uniforms. By midcentury, women began wearing shorter skirts for walking out of doors and made laced boots or ankle-high boots with inserts of elastic at the side quite fashionable. Men and

Men and women living in the nineteenth century enjoyed a variety of footwear, including oxfords like these. *Reproduced by permission of © Lake County Museum/CORBIS.*

$5

E.M.Scarbrough & Sons
Authentic
~ *Fall Shoe Fashions* ~

women needing less sturdy footwear wore leather and cloth shoes fastened with ties or buttons. For athletes, the first shoes made specifically for tennis appeared during this century. Delicate flat-soled leather or satin slippers were preferred by both men and women for formal events and evening wear for most of the century. However, both men and women began to replace their slippers with heeled satin pumps, or heeled slip-on shoes, at weddings and other formal occasions by the end of the century.

FOR MORE INFORMATION

Bigelow, Marybelle S. *Fashion in History: Apparel in the Western World.* Minneapolis, MN: Burgess Publishing, 1970.

Cosgrave, Bronwyn. *The Complete History of Costume and Fashion: From Ancient Egypt to the Present Day.* New York: Checkmark Books, 2000.

Payne, Blanche, Geitel Winakor, and Jane Farrell-Beck. *The History of Costume.* 2nd ed. New York: HarperCollins, 1992.

Boots

A variety of boot styles were popular during the nineteenth century. Half boots, or those reaching halfway to the knee, with square toes were commonly worn by men and ankle boots by women in the early years of the century. By the middle of the century, the British queen Victoria (1819–1901) popularized congress gaiters, leather ankle boots with elastic sewn into the side, among both men and women. The side-laced boots women wore under their long skirts became quite fashionable when they were suddenly visible underneath Bloomer outfits and shorter walking skirts in the later half of the century.

Tall boots made of leather or cloth were also fashionable for men. Men wore boots most often while outdoors and wore their trousers or breeches either tucked inside the boots' tall uppers or pulled over the tops and fastened with straps beneath the arch. Three styles were especially popular among fashionable men: Hussars, a military style of riding boots named after various European military units, were modeled on those worn by the Hungarian light cavalry of the fifteenth century; Hessians, thick leather boots trimmed below the knee with a tassel hanging from the center of the boot top, were named after a style worn by Germans from Hesse; and Wellingtons, boots covering the knee in front and cut lower in back for ease of movement, were made fashionable by the Duke of Wellington (1769–1852), the British military hero who defeated the French emperor Napoleon Bonaparte (1769–1821) in 1815 and became prime minister of Britain in 1828.

FOR MORE INFORMATION

Bigelow, Marybelle S. *Fashion in History: Apparel in the Western World.* Minneapolis, MN: Burgess Publishing, 1970.

Payne, Blanche, Geitel Winakor, and Jane Farrell-Beck. *The History of Costume.* 2nd ed. New York: HarperCollins, 1992.

■ Buttoned Shoes

Women's fashions during the mid- to late nineteenth century tended to emphasize modesty and covered the entire body with long flowing skirts and large puffed sleeves. Despite the modest nature of fashions, high-button shoes that became a fashion necessity for the women of the mid- to late 1800s demonstrated a bit of flirtatious fun. Button shoes and boots were made of leather or a combination of leather and fabric. They rose to the ankle or higher and fastened at the side with a long row of tiny buttons, sometimes made of semi-precious materials like white pearls. Because the long, wide skirts of the day hid a woman's shape completely, a lady's shoe might be the only visible part of the lower half of her body.

Buttoned shoes were closed with the aid of a special tool called a buttonhook, which was a long handle with a small hook at the end. Often beautifully crafted of fine

High-buttoned shoes, which rose to the ankle or higher and fastened with a long row of tiny buttons, became a fashion necessity for women of the mid- to late 1800s. *Reproduced by permission of © Gilbert Patrick/ CORBIS SYGMA.*

materials, the buttonhook was as important to a lady's dressing routine as hairpins and a comb. Once the shoes were on the feet, the hook was threaded through each small buttonhole, then hooked around the button and pulled back out, buttoning the shoe.

These high-buttoned shoes and boots concealed the feet completely with proper Victorian modesty, but they fit tightly, revealing the delicate shape of the foot to any who might be lucky enough to catch a glimpse of it beneath swishing skirts.

FOR MORE INFORMATION

Bigelow, Marybelle S. *Fashion in History: Western Dress, Prehistoric to Present.* Minneapolis, MN: Burgess Publishing, 1970.

Slippers, similar to these worn during the sixteenth century, adorned the feet of both fashionable men and women at parties and formal evening events during the nineteenth century. *Reproduced by permission of © Historical Picture Archive/ CORBIS.*

Cu moys de map le Jour sixiesme.
Mille cinq cens et le troisiesme.
Fut acheuee et parfaite.
Ceste translation. Et faite.
Dedens Rouen la bonne ville.
A tous lisans soit elle vtille.

Slippers

Slippers adorned the feet of both fashionable men and women at parties and formal evening events during the nineteenth century. Slippers were delicate foot coverings made of fabric, often satin, or soft leather. The uppers of slippers covered the heel and toes but left the top of the foot exposed. Slippers could slip on the foot or be secured with laces. Men wore black leather slippers trimmed at the toe with bows or ribbon roses for formal occasions. Women's slippers looked much like ballerina slippers with ties of leather or ribbon around the ankle. Women wore slippers in solid or two-toned colors that complimented their outfits. The delicacy of slippers required that they be worn only indoors, and by the end of the century satin pumps, heeled slip-on shoes, began to replace slippers as dress shoes for both men and women.

FOR MORE INFORMATION

Lister, Margot. *Costume: An Illustrated Survey from Ancient Times to the Twentieth Century.* London, England: Herbert Jenkins, 1967.

Payne, Blanche, Geitel Winakor, and Jane Farrell-Beck. *The History of Costume.* 2nd ed. New York: HarperCollins, 1992.

Tennis Shoes

Tennis shoes were lightweight canvas shoes with rubber soles, first introduced during the last half of the nineteenth century. They made their appearance just as many social sports were becoming fashionable and immediately became popular among active young people. Though often called tennis shoes after the sport that was also rising in popularity during the late 1800s, the canvas sports shoes have been given many other names, such as plimsolls, sneakers, trainers, and even felony shoes, because the rubber soles permit a quiet get-away for criminals.

Lightweight leather boots had been used for most sports until a scientific discovery in the mid-1800s paved the way for the introduction of a new kind of sports shoe. Charles Goodyear (1800–1860), an American rubber manufacturer, came up with a process for heating rubber called vulcanization. Vulcanization made rubber more flexible and stronger, and also enabled it to attach permanently to other materials, such as fabric. Once this new rubber was available shoe manufacturers began to use it to create new types of rubber soles. In 1868 a sturdy canvas and rubber shoe was introduced. The makers of the shoe called it a croquet sandal and recommended it for the lawn game croquet, played with balls and mallets, that was popular among fashionable young people of the upper classes.

The croquet sandal sold for six dollars a pair, a price too high for most working people to afford, so the new shoe was mainly worn by the wealthy at first. However, in 1873, the Sears and Roebuck Catalog began to offer a lace-up, rubber-soled canvas sports shoe for only sixty cents a pair, and the tennis shoe was on its way to mass popularity. In 1893, the influential fashion magazine *Vogue* reported on the popularity of the stylish new canvas sports shoe for ladies.

The late 1800s were marked by a widespread interest in such sports as croquet, tennis, and golf, all of which were played by both men and women. In Britain, women even began to play the national bat and ball game, cricket. The new canvas and rubber shoe, lightweight and sure-footed, was perfect for all of these games. In England the new shoes were called plimsolls, or plimmies, because the lines on the sides of the rubber sole looked like plimsoll lines which were painted on the sides of ships to show how heavy the ship was allowed to be loaded. (Samuel Plimsoll was the government minister who first decided the weight limits of ships.) In the United States, the name varied according to location, with tennis shoes or "tennies" being popular in the southeast, and sneakers in the northeast.

FOR MORE INFORMATION

Batterberry, Michael, and Ariane Batterberry. *Fashion: The Mirror of History.* New York: Greenwich House, 1977.

Vanderbilt, Tom. *The Sneaker Book: Anatomy of an Industry and an Icon.* New York: New Press, 1998.

Young, Robert. *Sneakers: The Shoes We Choose!* Minneapolis, MN: Dillon Press, 1991.

[*See also* **Volume 5, 1961–79: Tennis Shoes**]

Where to Learn More

■ ■ ■

The following list of resources focuses on material appropriate for middle school or high school students. Please note that Web site addresses were verified prior to publication but are subject to change.

BOOKS

Batterberry, Michael, and Ariane Batterberry. *Fashion: The Mirror of History.* New York: Greenwich House, 1977.

Bigelow, Marybelle S. *Fashion in History: Apparel in the Western World.* Minneapolis, MN: Burgess Publishing, 1970.

Boucher, François. *20,000 Years of Fashion: The History of Costume and Personal Adornment.* Extended ed. New York: Harry N. Abrams, 1987.

Contini, Mila. *Fashion: From Ancient Egypt to the Present Day.* Edited by James Laver. New York: Odyssey Press, 1965.

Corson, Richard. *Fashions in Hair: The First Five Thousand Years.* London, England: Peter Owen, 2001.

Cosgrave, Bronwyn. *The Complete History of Costume and Fashion: From Ancient Egypt to the Present Day.* New York: Checkmark Books, 2000.

Ewing, Elizabeth; revised and updated by Alice Mackrell. *History of Twentieth Century Fashion.* Lanham, MD: Barnes and Noble Books, 1992.

Hoobler, Dorothy, and Thomas Hoobler. *Vanity Rules: A History of American Fashion and Beauty.* Brookfield, CT: Twenty-First Century Books, 2000.

Laver, James. *Costume and Fashion: A Concise History.* 4th ed. London, England: Thames and Hudson, 2002.

Lawlor, Laurie. *Where Will This Shoe Take You?: A Walk through the History of Footwear.* New York: Walker and Co., 1996.

Lister, Margot. *Costume: An Illustrated Survey from Ancient Times to the Twentieth Century.* London, England: Herbert Jenkins, 1967.

Miller, Brandon Marie. *Dressed for the Occasion: What Americans Wore 1620-1970.* Minneapolis, MN: Lerner Publications, 1999.

Mulvagh, Jane. *Vogue History of 20th Century Fashion.* New York: Viking, 1988.

Payne, Blanche, Geitel Winakor, and Jane Farrell-Beck. *The History of Costume.* 2nd ed. New York: HarperCollins, 1992.

Peacock, John. *The Chronicle of Western Fashion: From Ancient Times to the Present Day.* New York: Harry N. Abrams, 1991.

Perl, Lila. *From Top Hats to Baseball Caps, from Bustles to Blue Jeans: Why We Dress the Way We Do.* New York: Clarion Books, 1990.

Pratt, Lucy, and Linda Woolley. *Shoes.* London, England: V&A Publications, 1999.

Racinet, Auguste. *The Historical Encyclopedia of Costumes.* New York: Facts on File, 1988.

Ribeiro, Aileen. *The Gallery of Fashion.* Princeton, NJ: Princeton University Press, 2000.

Rowland-Warne, L. *Costume.* New York: Dorling Kindersley, 2000.

Schnurnberger, Lynn Edelman. *Let There Be Clothes: 40,000 Years of Fashion.* New York: Workman, 1991.

Schoeffler, O. E., and William Gale. *Esquire's Encyclopedia of 20th Century Men's Fashions.* New York: McGraw-Hill, 1973.

Sichel, Marion. *History of Men's Costume.* New York: Chelsea House, 1984.

Steele, Valerie. *Fifty Years of Fashion: New Look to Now.* New Haven, CT: Yale University Press, 1997.

Trasko, Mary. *Daring Do's: A History of Extraordinary Hair.* New York: Flammarion, 1994.

Yarwood, Doreen. *The Encyclopedia of World Costume.* New York: Charles Scribner's Sons, 1978.

Yarwood, Doreen. *Fashion in the Western World, 1500–1990.* New York: Drama Book Publishers, 1992.

WEB SITES

Bender, A. *La Couturière Parisienne.* http://marquise.de/index.html (accessed on September 10, 2003).

Kathie Rothkop Hair Design. *Hair History.* http://www.hairrific.com/hist.htm (accessed on September 10, 2003).

Ladnier, Penny D. Dunlap. *The Costume Gallery.* http://www.costume gallery.com (accessed on September 10, 2003).

Maginnis, Tara. *The Costumer's Manifesto.* http://www.costumes.org/ (accessed on September 10, 2003).

Metropolitan Museum of Art. *The Costume Institute.* http://www. metmuseum.org/collections/department.asp?dep=8 (accessed on September 10, 2003).

Museum of Costume, Bath. http://www.museumofcostume.co.uk (accessed on September 10, 2003).

Sardo, Julie Zetterberg. *The Costume Page: Costuming Resources Online.* http://members.aol.com/nebula5/costume.html (accessed on September 10, 2003).

Thomas, Pauline Weston, and Guy Thomas. *Fashion-Era.* http://www. fashion-era.com/index.htm (accessed on September 10, 2003).

Index

∎ ∎ ∎

Italic type indicates volume number; **boldface** type indicates main entries and then page numbers; (ill.) indicates photos and illustrations.

A

B

C

D

H

I

J

L

▌▌ M

Q

R

T

X

Y

Z